Coming & Going

Lent Reflections

Jill Baker

Contents

Week 3: Fasting and Feasting

Week 4: Rejection

Preface

The Lord is your keeper;
   the Lord is your shade at your right hand.
The sun shall not strike you by day,
   nor the moon by night.
The Lord will keep you from all evil;
   he will keep your life.
The Lord will keep your going out and your
   coming in from this time on and for evermore.

                      Psalm 121:5-8

From the time that Andrew and I first began the process of offering for overseas service with the Methodist Church, I think we knew that if we were called to go abroad, we were also called to come back again! That may sound obvious, but it is a truth which was very significant to us in different ways over our eight years in the Caribbean. At first, perhaps, when we were still adjusting to the huge culture shock and many things seemed very strange, the knowledge that we would one day return to the UK was a comfort. Later, however, and increasingly so as our final two years in Grenada sped past so rapidly, the thought filled us with dread. St. Vincent and then Grenada had become our home, our sons, Timothy and Peter were happy in school; we had all made close and precious friendships – to return to Britain now would feel like 'leaving home', not like 'coming home'. At this time we had to remind each other frequently of our initial conviction that God was not inviting us to live in a new culture for our own sakes alone, but also so that we could learn from that culture and share new insights with our families and friends and with the church back in the UK.

So it is that this little collection of stories and reflections is called *Coming & Going*. When I wrote *Here & There*, a collection of Advent reflections, 'here' was the Caribbean, 'there' was Britain. Now that situation is reversed; our lives have gone through another 'going' and another 'coming'. Our return to life in Britain has been as much of a culture shock as was our move to St. Vincent, particularly for our boys who are, in many ways, West Indians. I would like to thank the people of the Stoke (South) Circuit of the Methodist Church who have done so much to ease us back into life 'here' and who have listened patiently to our many tales of life 'there'! Thank you Andrew, Timothy and Peter for letting me write about you all, and Sarah and Chris for your sterling work as 'guinea pigs' during Lent 2002.

You will notice that on some days, only selected verses from the Bible passage are printed; if possible, try to find time to read the full story. If you are using this book in a weekly study group, I hope you will find that the Bible passages raise their own questions for you. There are also a few possible discussion questions included for each week's theme.

I hope and pray that God will speak to all of us through his Word, as we walk the journey of faith this Lent and at all times. As we seek to serve him and make him known in his world, may we be blessed in our going out and in our coming in.

Jill Baker
Stoke-on-Trent
November 2002

Introduction: Come and see!

Throughout the Bible, from Adam and Eve in the garden to the closing verses of Revelation, God has been saying 'Come'. In modern Christian history, too, many have heard God's invitation to 'Come' in many different ways. As Lent begins, I believe God is saying to all who will listen, 'Come and see!'

Ash Wednesday   John 1:35-42
　　'What are you looking for?'

Thursday   Isaiah 55:1-3a
　　Everyone who thirsts, come . . .

Friday   John 1:43-49
　　He found Philip . . . Philip found Nathanael

Saturday   Hosea 6:1-3
　　'Come, let us return to the Lord'

Ash Wednesday   John 1:35-42
'What are you looking for?'

The next day John again was standing with two of his disciples, and as he watched Jesus walk by, he exclaimed, 'Look, here is the Lamb of God!' The two disciples heard him say this and they followed Jesus. When Jesus turned and saw them following, he said to them, 'What are you looking for?' They said to him, 'Rabbi' (which translated means Teacher), 'where are you staying?' He said to them, 'Come and see.' They came and saw where he was staying, and they remained with him that day. It was about four o'clock in the afternoon. One of the two who heard John speak and followed him was Andrew, Simon Peter's brother. He first found his brother Simon and said to him, 'We have found the Messiah' (which is translated Anointed). He brought Simon to Jesus, who looked at him and said, 'You are Simon son of John. You are to be called Cephas' (which is translated Peter).

Invitations are always exciting to receive. Being invited somewhere makes us feel wanted, included, important to someone else. One of the most unusual invitations Andrew and I received while working as mission partners in St. Vincent in the South Caribbean was from two teenage girls in the church youth fellowship inviting us to the wedding of their parents – what a happy day of celebration that was! Living abroad, four thousand miles from family and friends, we were always delighted when someone said, 'We'd like you to come to our home', and we enjoyed so many kinds of hospitality over the eight years. One older lady wanted everything to be very English for us, and served us tea in bone china cups – probably made in the Potteries where we now live and work – with slices of cake, and even presented us with her collection of pictures of the Queen! Others chose to share with us the best of Caribbean cuisine and so we acquired a taste for saltfish and breadfruit, cow heel soup, 'oildown' (Grenada's national dish) and learned to crack crab's claws between our teeth to enjoy crab and callaloo in the proper way!

Being overseas in itself was, for us, very much a response to an invitation from God. During training for the Methodist ministry, Andrew felt increasingly stirred by the stories told him of years of service in China by two older women in our congregation. As he relayed the stories to me, I was at first interested in their experiences, then horrified as I realised what lay behind the telling of these tales, but, ultimately, excited by the feeling that God was saying to us, 'Come and see what I am doing in another part of my world.'

Throughout the pages of the Bible, God issues invitations to women and men, girls and boys. In today's reading we see his immediate offer of hospitality to two of John the Baptist's disciples; his home was open to them and they stayed with him all day . . . how wonderful to be a fly on the wall on that occasion! Notice the only question Jesus asks the two before inviting them in: 'What are you looking for?' He doesn't check up on their level of income, their standing in the town, their academic qualifications or their reputation as Jewish believers. All he asks is if they are looking for something or someone. As Lent begins, I believe we may all hear God speaking these same words to us, 'What are you looking for?' What is your life about? What is important to you? What do you feel you lack? Where is your life shallow and trivial? Are you in need of peace, security, forgiveness, love? If we feel we are not looking for anything in life, then we may miss the invitation which Jesus still offers, 'Come and see.'

Prayer:

Lord Jesus, I hear you now challenging me about my life. I can't face the pressures and problems of life on my own. Like those two disciples, I want to be wherever you are. Thank you for inviting me to come and see – give me grace to walk this journey which will join my life to yours as I see where you are at work in your world and in me today. Amen

Thursday   Isaiah 55:1-3a
Everyone who thirsts, come . . .

Ho, everyone who thirsts, come to the waters;
    and you that have no money, come, buy and eat!
Come, buy wine and milk without money
    and without price.
Why do you spend your money for that
    which is not bread,
        and your labour for that which does not satisfy?
Listen carefully to me, and eat what is good, and delight
    yourselves in rich food.
Incline your ear, and come to me; listen, so that
    you may live.

'Thirst' took on a completely new meaning for me when we began living in the Caribbean! Our younger son, Peter, was only fourteen weeks old when we exchanged an English January for the heat of St. Vincent – did he wonder what had suddenly happened to turn his life upside down? Probably he did, and he expressed his perplexity by the need to feed almost constantly. In turn, I was perpetually thirsty and in those early days and nights could not get enough to drink. A few months later we made our first ascent of the volcano in Chateaubelair – La Soufrière. It was a scorching day and we had not taken enough water; we gave all we could to the children. Andrew and I reached home desperate for fluid and we rapidly emptied the fridge of the many bottles of cooled, boiled water we always kept there!

God's invitation through Isaiah is to all who are thirsty or hungry to come and be satisfied, to drink water, wine and milk, to eat bread, rich food and all that is good. And as if that were not enough in itself; there is to be no charge for this banquet; no money is needed, all is freely provided. It sounds too good to be true. So do we believe it? Do we believe that God has the resources to satisfy our deepest needs, to quench the hunger and thirst of our souls? Or do we rather believe the consumerist gospel of the day which tells us that it is having possessions which satisfies us; which encourages us to insure ourselves against every eventuality so that we might feel secure; which promotes leisure and pleasure as the true routes to happiness? We go along with this philosophy at our peril, for it is a lie. Listen again to the yearning voice of God, speaking directly to us today from almost three thousand years ago, 'Why do you spend your money for that which is not bread, and your labour for that which does not satisfy?'

As I reflect on the past eight years spent in a different culture, I call to mind so many folk who had discovered that the secret of abundant life lay not in accumulating money to spend in the shops, but in recognising the hunger and thirst of their souls and coming to the living waters of Jesus Christ to be refreshed, filled and satisfied. At the start of Lent, there is a challenge here to us all. Yesterday we faced the question, 'What are you looking for?' Today we need to ask ourselves whether we know what it means to be hungry and thirsty for God. Are we setting out on this Lenten journey with a deep desire to know more of God? Have we recognised that much of what we have been spending our money on is not bread at all, since it has no power to strengthen us or help us to grow? Can we face the possibility that what we have been labouring for will never satisfy us? If we can, then we are promised a rich banquet in the coming weeks as we learn to listen to the words of God: 'Listen, so that you may live.'

Prayer:

Lord God, you are the source of all abundant life, the fountain of living waters, the Bread of Life. As I come to you today I confess that I have so often tried to slake my thirst at the wrong spring and have taken the edge off my hunger for you by my appetite for that which is not bread. Thank you for your invitation to come to your waters, to sit at your banquet and to receive from you the life for which my spirit longs. I am coming, Lord. Amen

Friday   John 1:43-49
He found Philip . . . Philip found Nathanael

The next day Jesus decided to go to Galilee. He found Philip and said to him, 'Follow me.' Now Philip was from Bethsaida, the city of Andrew and Peter. Philip found Nathanael and said to him, 'We have found him about whom Moses in the law and also the prophets wrote, Jesus son of Joseph from Nazareth.' Nathanael said to him, 'Can anything good come out of Nazareth?' Philip said to him, 'Come and see.' When Jesus saw Nathanael coming towards him, he said of him, 'Here is truly an Israelite in whom there is no deceit!' Nathanael asked him, 'Where did you come to know me?' Jesus answered, 'I saw you under the fig tree before Philip called you.' Nathanael replied, 'Rabbi, you are the Son of God! You are the King of Israel!'

These verses follow on immediately from the reading we looked at on Ash Wednesday. After being called to follow Jesus, Philip seeks out his friend, Nathanael, to tell him what he has discovered. When confronted with Nathanael's prejudice against the little Northern town of Nazareth, Philip replies with the very same words that Jesus spoke to others the day before, 'Come and see'.

Not many of us find it easy in the post-Christian, secular culture of Britain in the twenty-first century to speak freely to others of what we have found in Jesus. We hesitate even to invite friends to 'come and see' for themselves, by attending worship at church, a Bible study group or prayer meeting. Perhaps I notice this all the more having recently returned to live and work in Britain. Our reticence contrasts strikingly with the open, unembarrassed declarations of faith in and love for God which flowed freely amongst our Caribbean sisters and brothers.

An observation made by a British Methodist minister who visited us in St. Vincent was that, by comparison, the British

Church had lost its confidence. If this is true, we need to ask: in what have we lost confidence? In ourselves? Surely that is all to the good, for the message of the entire Bible is that, left alone, humankind repeatedly runs into disaster. In the Church and its structures? Maybe that is not such a bad thing either, for Church history too is littered with shameful incidents and regrettable divisions. In God? There lies the crux of the question, for if we have lost confidence in God, we will be too afraid to face the Goliaths of our age, just as Saul was.

There is no doubt that there is a huge gap today between 'the pavement and the pew', and every church and every Christian needs to address the issue of crossing that gap. Perhaps it helps to remind ourselves that Jesus already knows intimately those whom we long to reach. Even when we have shut ourselves away in safe enclaves, losing contact with the youth culture of the day for fear that it will somehow defile us, Jesus has not. The last few verses of our reading show us how Jesus knew all about Nathanael even while Nathanael was still sceptical about him. What is more, he was able to speak to him in such a way that, within moments of their meeting, Nathanael confessed Jesus as Son of God and King of Israel!

As we hear Jesus calling us to 'Come and see' this Lent, maybe we, like Philip, will also be inspired to pass on that invitation to others in our circle of family, friends and neighbours. How we do so will depend on many things – on the sort of person we are, on the opportunities available to us, on the needs of the person to whom we speak – but in every situation we *can* have confidence in Jesus.

Prayer:

Lord Jesus, you know how often I hesitate to speak your name as I talk to those around me. You know this, and yet you do not reject me as worthless. Give me grace, I pray, so to live and breathe and speak for you that others may see you at work in me. Lord, I believe, help my unbelief! Amen

Saturday   Hosea 6:1-3
'Come, let us return to the Lord'

'Come, let us return to the Lord; for it is he who has torn,
   and he will heal us;
     he has struck down, and he will bind us up.
After two days he will revive us;
   on the third day he will raise us up, that we may live
   before him.
Let us know, let us press on to know the Lord;
   his appearing is as sure as the dawn;
     he will come to us like the showers,
like the spring rains that water the earth.'

➢ This passage, along with the others chosen for the Saturdays of Lent, is selected more as a springboard for our meditation than for the kind of study and reflection we engage in on other days.

➢ Many of us have different routines at weekends, when there are no school buses to catch, packed lunches to make or office deadlines to meet – we may even hope for a lie-in!

➢ In the Caribbean, Saturday is generally washing day, and – for many – the busiest day for selling or buying in the market, so an early start is essential.

➢ For folk on their own, Saturday can be a very lonely day; families are caught up in their own activities and no one comes to call.

➢ Whatever our routines, let us try during Lent to make some time for meditation.

➢ If possible, read the passage several times during the day, letting the words make their home in your heart, then sit down quietly towards the end of the day and allow God to speak through his Word. This can be a wonderful preparation for Sunday worship tomorrow.

He has torn / he has struck down . . .

Where and when have I been torn and struck down in life? Has God done this to me? Why? Why has God allowed these times to happen?

And he will heal / he will bind us up . . .

Do I trust God for this? Has my healing begun already? Am I resisting this healing or opening myself to it?

After two days / on the third day . . .

Time between: the space between Good Friday and Easter Day. Why? For what purpose? For what possible purpose in my life?

Let us press on to know the Lord . . .

What am I planning this Lent that will lead me in this way? How can I press on to know the Lord? Can I do this on my own, or do I need to be part of an 'us'?

His appearing is as sure as the dawn / he will come to us . . .

Do I have or can I have this sort of trust in God? What prevents me from having confidence in Jesus?

Like the showers / like the spring rains . . .

In the British climate we are not always as glad to see rain as are many parts of the world . . . think of a cooling shower on a dusty hot day, or spring rains setting off the growth of so many hidden plants . . . are parts of my life dry and dusty? Do I need awakening, refreshing, watering?

Questions:

1. At the start of Lent, what are you looking for? In what areas of your life do you need to hear Jesus' invitation to 'Come and see'?

2. What are the questions people outside the church are asking today? Are any of your neighbours and friends asking the sort of questions to which you could reply, 'Come and see'? How do you respond?

3. Reflecting on your own life at present, do you think you are 'spending money on that which is not bread, or labour for that which does not satisfy'? How can this situation be changed?

Week 1: Surprises!

Some years ago, a friend who had recently returned from working as a mission partner in Africa commented to us that, in comparison, church worship in Britain seemed 'clockwork'. Of course, this is not the whole picture, but there is always a danger that our church structures and practices run themselves so smoothly that God is squeezed out of the picture. Perhaps the Church in the West needs to 'loosen up' a bit and regain some of the spontaneity of the early Primitive Methodists, whose revival had its roots in and around the Potteries, where I now live. Perhaps, in our church order and patterns of worship, we need to allow God to be God, to let the leading of God's Holy Spirit control the way we do things, rather than the other way round. Do we tend to think up schemes, be they for building projects, social activities or outreach programmes and then ask God to 'bless' them, or do we wait upon God for his inspiration?

During this first full week of Lent we look at some stories with surprises, or even shocks, for those involved.

First Sunday in Lent John 2:1-11
   Good wine

Monday Exodus 34:27-29
   The skin of his face shone

Tuesday Ruth 4:13-17
   The restorer of life

Wednesday 2 Samuel 9:1, 3b-8
   He fell on his face

Thursday John 11:38-44
   See the glory of God!

Friday Acts 10:9-16
   By no means, Lord!

Saturday 2 Corinthians 5:16-21
   Everything has become new!

First Sunday in Lent   John 2:1-11
Good wine

On the third day there was a wedding in Cana of Galilee, and the mother of Jesus was there. Jesus and his disciples had also been invited to the wedding. When the wine gave out, the mother of Jesus said to him, 'They have no wine.' And Jesus said to her, 'Woman, what concern is that to you and to me? My hour has not yet come.' His mother said to the servants, 'Do whatever he tells you.' Now standing there were six stone water-jars for the Jewish rites of purification, each holding twenty or thirty gallons. Jesus said to them, 'Fill the jars with water.' And they filled them up to the brim. He said to them, 'Now draw some out and take it to the chief steward.' So they took it. When the steward tasted the water that had become wine, and did not know where it came from (though the servants who had drawn the water knew), the steward called the bridegroom and said to him, 'Everyone serves the good wine first, and then the inferior wine after the guests have become drunk. But you have kept the good wine until now.' Jesus did this, the first of his signs, in Cana in Galilee, and revealed his glory; and his disciples believed in him.

On this first Sunday in Lent, when our church lectionary directs our thoughts to Jesus fasting in the wilderness, perhaps it seems rather strange to focus on this story of feasting and celebration. However, Sundays were never considered to be fast days in church practice, and are not counted in the forty days of Lent itself.

When we look behind the familiarity of many Bible stories, both in the Old and New Testaments, we find a God who often acts in a surprising way. I have found this to be true in my own life – neither Andrew nor I had ever sought after the 'sun, sea, sand' kind of holiday, but after offering to the Methodist Church Overseas Division (as it then was) we found ourselves spending almost eight years on small Caribbean islands! In many ways – large and small – God is waiting to surprise us as we allow our lives to be directed by the Holy Spirit.

In this story, Jesus says clearly to his mother that the shortage of wine is not their problem; yet it seems that Mary knows her son well enough to believe that he would still act, and she tells the servants to do whatever he tells them. Thus a vast quantity of superior wine is suddenly found on the menu, and even the wine steward is impressed when he tastes it. Perhaps the quality of the wine is, for us, the least surprising element of the story, for we know from the earliest pages of the Bible that what God does, he does well. 'And God saw that it was good' becomes the chorus of each day's work of creation in Genesis 1.

What about our lives? Can we say that the touch of God's hand upon our lives has transformed us into something fragrant and sparkling, bringing pleasure to those around us? Or do we feel more like a jar of flat, colourless water, or – possibly even worse – has our attitude to life become sour, like a bottle of cheap wine gone stale? This story challenges us deeply about how we live our lives; about how we demonstrate to the world what God is able to do with the ordinary material of our day-to-day living, as Paul elaborates in 1 Corinthians 1:26-31. The story can also give us great hope for it tells us that God is always waiting in the wings to do something new and surprising with us. As we walk our Lenten path of devotion, let us not come to God with a list of what we want, but let us open our lives for him to surprise us.

Prayer:

Lord God of surprises, just as you surprised Moses and Ruth, David and Deborah, Paul, Mary and so many others, surprise me, I pray. Work in my life and in my church so that others may want to taste and see how good you are; reveal your glory that others may believe, for Jesus' sake. Amen

Monday   Exodus 34:27-29
The skin of his face shone

The Lord said to Moses: Write these words; in accordance with these words I have made a covenant with you and with Israel. He was there with the Lord forty days and forty nights; he neither ate bread nor drank water. And he wrote on the tablets the words of the covenant, the ten commandments. Moses came down from Mount Sinai. As he came down from the mountain with the two tablets of the covenant in his hand, Moses did not know that the skin of his face shone because he had been talking with God.

During our time in St. Vincent, a young woman with three daughters came to live in Chateaubelair; she had been living with a Rastafarian man for a number of years and whilst she had not adopted his beliefs, she and her daughters all wore their hair in the dreadlocks associated with that lifestyle. I first met her when she came to the gate of the manse asking if I could give her something for one daughter's skin condition – a lumpy rash caused, the mother believed, by eating too many green mangoes! I am not a nurse, but was glad to meet this family, to talk and pray with them and to hear something of their story. Over the following weeks, as various members of the church befriended the woman and her girls, a transformation began to take place, marked outwardly one Sunday morning when, to the surprise of many in the congregation, she brought her youngest two daughters to church for baptism – without the distinctive dreadlocks! Her outward appearance was utterly changed, but as everyone was well aware, the cutting of her own and her girls' hair was much, much more than a change of fashion. It was, rather, a statement about the new direction her life was taking – a life now centred on Christ.

When Moses returned from forty days and nights on Mount Sinai with God, following immediately after his encounter with the glory of God's back whilst hidden in the cleft of a rock (Exodus 33:17-23), his outward appearance too was transformed. Although he was unaware of it, the skin of his face shone so much that even his brother Aaron was afraid to come near him. We cannot read this story without thinking of another mountain-top experience when Jesus was transfigured and, Matthew tells us, 'his face shone like the sun' (Matthew 17:2). Again Moses was present and how his heart must have rejoiced as he saw the glory of God in the face of Christ and understood how God was continuing the process of revelation, in which he himself had been involved around fifteen centuries before!

This process continues . . . Stephen, in Acts 6:15, was observed to have 'the face of an angel'; Paul, picking up Moses' story in 2 Corinthians 3:18 says, 'And all of us, with unveiled faces, seeing the glory of the Lord as though reflected in a mirror, are being transformed into the same image from one degree of glory to another; for this comes from the Lord, the Spirit.' Moving to the end of the Bible, in Revelation 1:16-17, John encounters One whose face is 'like the sun shining with full force'. No cleft of the rock now, no veil, no condition of secrecy, no mirror – the revelation is full, final and blinding, and John falls down as though dead.

It's heady stuff, but it is also the stuff of our daily lives. Our God of surprises is still in the business of transformation, wanting to replace the fear in our lives with trust, the despair with hope, the worry with peace. According to the examples of Scripture the route to this transformation is simple – perhaps too simple for some of us – we must spend time with God. Like Peter and John we must be 'companions of Jesus' (Acts 4:13). Lent is a good time to find new routines in our daily lives which allow us to do just that.

Prayer:

Lord Jesus Christ, I confess that too often I do not display your glory in my face, in my mind or in my life, but I thank you that the work of transformation is not mine, but yours. Give me grace, I pray, that I too may be 'changed from glory into glory' until in heaven I see your face. Amen

Tuesday   Ruth 4:13-17
The restorer of life

So Boaz took Ruth and she became his wife. When they came together, the Lord made her conceive, and she bore a son. Then the women said to Naomi, 'Blessed be the Lord who has not left you this day without next-of-kin; and may his name be renowned in Israel! He shall be to you a restorer of life and a nourisher of your old age; for your daughter-in-law who loves you, who is more to you than seven sons, has borne him.' Then Naomi took the child and laid him in her bosom, and became his nurse. The women of the neighbourhood gave him a name, saying, 'A son has been born to Naomi.' They named him Obed; he became the father of Jesse, the father of David.

Not all stories in real life have fairy tale happy endings, but the story of Ruth certainly does. Not only for Ruth and Boaz who, we imagine, 'live happily ever after', but also for Ruth's mother-in-law Naomi, who, at the end of a life of displacement and sorrow, is fêted amongst the women of her community as she receives her grandson, the infant Obed, into her arms. Old age is increasingly seen as a problem, or at least as a challenge. Many older people feel hopeless and helpless as they consider the years ahead. There is a challenge to all Christians to develop a 'theology of old age' which takes account of a God of surprises, a God who always has something up his sleeve, a God who can give hope in the bleakest of circumstances.

Obed is described to Naomi as 'a restorer of life and a nourisher of your old age' for he has become her 'next-of-kin' with a responsibility to care and provide for her, a woman without other male relatives, in her old age. What a welcome surprise this must have been for Naomi, who had been in despair and depression as she returned to Bethlehem some time before, telling her old friends not to call her Naomi, meaning 'pleasant' but Mara, 'bitter' (Ruth 1:19-21).

What is our attitude as we contemplate the future? Some people have a clear-cut 'life-plan' in which every possible financial or physical need is accounted for; others refuse to think ahead or to countenance the possibility of ill-health or dependence – most of us are somewhere in between. Most parents of young people live with many worries about the pressures their teenage children face; many older people, like Naomi, wonder who will care for them when they can no longer care for themselves, and even children these days are not without their own stresses and anxieties as they try to make sense of a rapidly changing world. Since the tragic events of September 11th 2001 and its repercussions, many more people across the world feel increasingly uneasy about what the future may hold collectively as well as individually.

As Christians we are called to maintain our faith in a God who is faithful and can be trusted, but this must not become a vague hope for a 'fairy godmother' kind of God who at the end will wave her wand and make it all come right. One amazing transformation which we were so privileged to be involved with in Grenada was to see the New Hampshire Methodist Centre built on a piece of overgrown land in the heart of a small rural village – it didn't happen overnight! A vast amount of hard work and dedicated fund-raising by people in many parts of the world, inspired and enabled by God's Holy Spirit, led to a transformation which itself continues God's transforming work in that community. The infant Obed was unable to do anything at all for his grandmother as the story closes – there are years of love and training ahead if he is to fulfil all that is hoped of him. In him, however, lie the seeds of a peaceful and secure future, and not only for Naomi, for Obed is to become the grandfather of Israel's greatest king, David, and, through him, the ancestor of Jesus himself.

Prayer:

Lord of the future, God of surprises, you who are the true restorer of life and nourisher of our every age, I bring to you a world of worries – my own and those of my neighbour next door and my neighbour across the world. Open my eyes to see your seedlings of peace and security, that I may live a life of trust through which your name is renowned in my community.
Amen

Wednesday   2 Samuel 9:1, 3b-8
He fell on his face

David asked, 'Is there still anyone left of the house of Saul to whom I may show kindness for Jonathan's sake?' . . . Ziba said to the king, 'There remains a son of Jonathan; he is crippled in his feet.' The king said to him, 'Where is he?' Ziba said to the king, 'He is in the house of Machir son of Ammiel, at Lo-debar.' Then King David sent and brought him from the house of Machir son of Ammiel, at Lo-debar. Mephibosheth son of Jonathan son of Saul came to David, and fell on his face and did obeisance. David said, 'Mephibosheth!' He answered, 'I am your servant.' David said to him, 'Do not be afraid, for I will show you kindness for the sake of your father Jonathan; I will restore to you all the land of your grandfather Saul, and you yourself shall eat at my table always.' He did obeisance and said, 'What is your servant, that you should look upon a dead dog such as I am?'

When Mephibosheth received his summons to the presence of the new king, David, he doubtless thought that it would be his final journey. In order to secure their tenure of the throne, it was common practice for new kings to destroy all close living relations of the former king, and there could have been those amongst David's enemies who might have suggested that Mephibosheth, Saul's grandson, had a right to the kingship. We can only try to imagine the surprise Mephibosheth felt as he grovelled before David's feet and heard words of kindness and restoration! As the promise of his new life at the king's table opened up to him, Mephibosheth continued to do obeisance at David's feet, but with an entirely different motive in his heart!

At our final service in the Richmond Hill Prison in St. George's, one of the former leaders of the revolution tried to sum up what had been Andrew's message over his four years of ministry there. He spoke of three different approaches to God which he had observed amongst the many preachers and ministers he had heard during his life, both before and in prison. Some, he observed, preached of coming to God out of fear and to avoid punishment; others urged conversion in order to gain reward from God, but, he now saw, the only true response to God is one of grateful love.

What is our motive for worshipping God? We shall return to the question of motive in Holy Week, but Mephibosheth raises the question for us now. We might be unwilling to admit to fear as a motive for our attendance at worship week by week, but is there, in the back of our minds, a thought not unlike Mephibosheth's, that God is the rightful King who has many good reasons to destroy us utterly, and so we need to crave his mercy? Or have we allowed him to surprise us with his amazing love and goodness which not only save us from the death we deserve, but restore us to a full and abundant life, inviting us to sit and eat with him at his table?

May God forgive us all in the Christian Church that, over the centuries, has managed to blur and confuse the central message with which we have been entrusted, so that those outside the Church are more likely to believe that God stands ready to judge them than to accept that they are loved by him beyond their imagining.

Prayer:

Lord God, your unconditional, undeserved love for me is something which I still find hard to accept. So often I think I would rather earn my way into your favour. Help me, I pray, to understand more of your grace and mercy, that I may fall at your feet in humble thankfulness and receive as a crippled, wretched beggar all the riches you have for me. Amen

Thursday   John 11:38-44
See the glory of God!

Then Jesus, again greatly disturbed, came to the tomb. It was a cave, and a stone was lying against it. Jesus said, 'Take away the stone.' Martha, the sister of the dead man, said to him, 'Lord, already there is a stench because he has been dead four days.' Jesus said to her, 'Did I not tell you that if you believed you would see the glory of God?' So they took away the stone. And Jesus looked upward and said, 'Father, I thank you for having heard me. I knew that you always hear me, but I have said this for the sake of the crowd standing here, so that they may believe that you sent me.' When he had said this he cried with a loud voice, 'Lazarus, come out!' The dead man came out, his hands and feet bound with strips of cloth, and his face wrapped in a cloth. Jesus said to them, 'Unbind him, and let him go.'

After my much-loved uncle died, I remember the longing to see him walk into a room again, back into our lives . . . I am sure everyone who has been bereaved knows that longing. So our hearts rejoice with Martha and Mary, the two sisters of Lazarus, who received just such a marvellous surprise. For, despite the strong faith that both women had in Jesus, I am sure it *was* a surprise; I don't think either of them expected for a moment that Jesus would restore Lazarus to life. Earlier in the chapter (v24) Martha had expressed her belief in a resurrection 'on the last day', but her unwillingness to let Jesus open the tomb leads us to believe that she had no expectation of a resurrection on that particular day.

As Christians we know that we believe in a God of resurrection – the resurrection of Jesus is only the first fruits of what will be 'on the last day'. We are told that African slaves working on the plantations of the West Indies sang many songs telling of that glorious future when tears would be dried, pain would be defeated and justice restored. The words of these songs and the faith behind them still survive in the choruses which are sung regularly in chapels in which we worshipped in St. Vincent and Grenada: 'When the battle is over, we shall wear a crown', 'Won't it be a time, when we get over yonder', 'Soon and very soon, we're going to see the King' . . .

It is right for us to hold this kind of faith, but perhaps the story of Lazarus also teaches us to look for resurrection happening here and now, today. Having grown up in the Caribbean, our son Peter experienced his first autumn and winter at the age of eight – he had observed the leaves changing colour and falling with great interest, and one January morning asked the vital question, 'How will the trees get their leaves back?' What an excitement spring became as we all saw afresh the resurrection of snowdrops, daffodils, catkins, leaves, blossom . . !

However, before we get too carried away with the links between spring and Lent, we must remember that it is only in the temperate zones of the northern hemisphere that this tie-up occurs, and it is a throw-back to the dominance of that part of the world that the very name 'Lent' comes from an early English word for 'lengthening' – in other places the days are getting shorter as Easter approaches. Spring is a wonderful illustration of resurrection here and now, but it is not the only one; wherever past wrongs are forgiven, wherever relationships begin to grow again after a period of dormancy or decay, wherever people fight their way back from depression, addiction and other illnesses, wherever a heart which has been turned away from God turns back towards him, there is resurrection. May we be those who see and share this message of resurrection with all who are grieving for some sort of loss in our families, churches and communities.

Prayer:

> *As you spoke to Martha, Lord Jesus Christ, so I hear your voice speaking to me today, 'I am the resurrection and the life . . . do you believe this?' Give me faith, I pray, to believe and so to see the glory of God as your resurrection power is at work in my life and in your world.* Amen

Friday   Acts 10:9-16
By no means, Lord!

About noon the next day, as they were on their journey and approaching the city, Peter went up on the roof to pray. He became hungry and wanted something to eat; and while it was being prepared he fell into a trance. He saw the heaven opened and something like a large sheet coming down, being lowered to the ground by its four corners. In it were all kinds of four-footed creatures and reptiles and birds of the air. Then he heard a voice saying, 'Get up, Peter, kill and eat.' But Peter said, 'By no means, Lord; for I have never eaten anything that is profane or unclean.' The voice said to him again, a second time, 'What God has made clean, you must not call profane.' This happened three times, and the thing was suddenly taken up to heaven.

When Methodism began talking about a new hymn book I was vigorously opposed to the idea – the *Methodist Hymn Book* had become a friend through my childhood, and had been there for me in the questioning years of adolescence, seeing me through into my own faith-commitment. It contained much great theology and stirring music, and besides, I knew all the numbers! Why did we need a new book? I blush now at the arrogance of my arguments in my early twenties, a time when many of us feel we know all the answers! Of course I was wrong, and, thankfully, have been proved to be wrong by a wonderful explosion of new, Christian music and honest, challenging lyrics which enhance much of our worship.

It isn't easy admitting you are wrong, is it? Those of us like Peter (and me) who tend to speak before we think and to take very firm stands on any and every subject may find it particularly difficult (despite getting more practice at it!). Can we imagine Peter's horror at being presented with animals, reptiles and birds that he has been brought up to consider unclean, and hearing a voice, which he presumes to be God's, telling him to eat them? Does he think at first that God is testing him, finding out whether, like Daniel before him, he will remain faithful to the Jewish food laws in the face of temptation? Whatever he thinks, his answer is strong: 'By no means, Lord!' God, however, is not easily diverted; he repeats the instruction three times and then, while Peter is still wondering what it all means, messengers come from the Roman, Cornelius, and gradually God's message to Peter becomes plain. The animals were an illustration – this is the real thing; can Peter now respond with warmth and generosity to people he would formerly have considered to be unclean? Peter can, and does, and so the Christian mission to the Gentiles begins in earnest. It is worth noting (as the following chapters of Acts record, especially Acts 15) that this causes considerable heartache for Peter and the Early Church generally, as other leaders object strongly to such an 'open door' policy.

Perhaps some of us as Christians today, and some of our leaders within the Christian Church, are being called to look afresh at some of the practices and traditions we have held dear for many years and to find out whether God wants us to hold on to them or to be willing to cast them aside in order that his kingdom may be advanced? Church meeting agendas cover a wide spectrum of issues, from debates about seating arrangements, music and times of services to big questions about the future direction of some of our congregations or buildings. Whatever we are discussing, can we be sure we are not coming to God with the response, 'By no means, Lord!'? In our personal, devotional lives, too, let us look out for any 'No entry' signs we may be putting up to keep God out. Lent is a very appropriate time to begin looking for areas where it is just conceivable that we may be in the wrong!

Prayer:

Lord Jesus, your gospel is a disturbing message to many of us – we have built safe structures in which to be comfortable, but you are calling us out of them. Give us grace to respond, that we may not miss the opportunities you are offering. May we have the courage and faith to say, 'Yes, Lord, by all means.' Amen

Saturday   2 Corinthians 5:16-21
Everything has become new!

From now on, therefore, we regard no one from a human point of view; even though we once knew Christ from a human point of view, we know him no longer in that way. So if anyone is in Christ, there is a new creation: everything old has passed away; see, everything has become new! All this is from God, who reconciled us to himself through Christ, and has given us the ministry of reconciliation; that is, in Christ God was reconciling the world to himself, not counting their trespasses against them, and entrusting the message of reconciliation to us. So we are ambassadors for Christ, since God is making his appeal through us; we entreat you on behalf of Christ, be reconciled to God. For our sake he made him to be sin who knew no sin, so that in him we might become the righteousness of God.

We regard no one from a human point of view . . .
A call to see everyone through God's eyes – our husband/wife, our children/parents, our neighbours and work colleagues, as well as groups we may have little contact with but strong opinions about – the homeless, refugees, travellers, drug addicts, asylum seekers . . . and Christ himself, 'Just as you did it to one of the least of these . . . you did it to me.'

So if anyone is in Christ, there is a new creation . . .
In Christ what was impossible becomes possible.

Everything old has passed away . . .
What do I long to forget? What words and actions from the past still haunt me? Can I lay them aside; are they 'old' or are they really still part of me today?

See, everything has become new! . . .
New heart, new mind, new eyes, new attitudes . . .

All this is from God, who reconciled us to himself through Christ, and has given us the ministry of reconciliation . . .
Made in God's image, called to be like God and to do what God is doing in the world.

So we are ambassadors for Christ . . .
We cannot go on blaming those outside the Christian faith for misunderstanding Christ – it is the ambassadors who must present the real picture.

Since God is making his appeal through us; we entreat you on behalf of Christ, be reconciled to God . . .
The real picture of a vulnerable God in Christ, appealing to all, 'Come back to me.'

For our sake he made him to be sin who knew no sin, so that in him we might become the righteousness of God . . .
Of course we are sinful, of course we are weak and selfish, of course we fail, but in Christ God has provided a remedy for sin, and offers us a position of righteousness – not, thankfully, self-righteousness, but the righteousness of God.

Questions:

1. Sparking or still? (or even sour?) Does your life and your church express the 'abundant life' which Jesus came to give to his followers, or would non-church – goers be justified in saying, 'this is dead'?

2. Most Methodist congregations in the UK have a relatively high average age. Is there a 'theology of old age'? Is there still the possibility of abundant life where sickness and senility leave their cruel marks?

3. What are the signs of resurrection around us – in our lives, our communities and our churches? How can we demonstrate this resurrection to a grieving, lost world?

4. Have you ever been wrong? (!) Is it possible that you, or your church, are getting something wrong at the moment? How can Peter's story (see Friday) help us to change when God requires us to?

Week 2: Breaking out!

Many of us as Christians wrestle with stories in the Bible – particularly the Old Testament – which seem to portray God as vengeful, even capricious. We don't like to read of massacres in battle, or plagues sent as punishments or innocent women and children killed because of the sin of their menfolk. These hard questions have no easy answers, but perhaps our perspective on such happenings can be changed if we take more seriously God's holy nature and his abhorrence of human sin. Like the volcanoes, earthquakes and other devastating phenomena which occur when two of the earth's tectonic plates clash, the meeting of holiness and sin has to produce a reaction. No wonder the sky went dark on Good Friday, no wonder Jesus shouted out, 'My God, my God, why have you forsaken me?' as the full weight of human sin separated him from the holiness of God. No wonder we read, in both Old and New Testaments, of God breaking out . . .

Second Sunday in Lent   John 2:13-17
    In the temple he found . . .

Monday   Genesis 19:15-26
    Flee for your life

Tuesday
    An image of a calf   Exodus 32:7-10

Wednesday
    The Lord burst forth   2 Samuel 6:1-11

Thursday
    Woe to you . . . hypocrites!   Matthew 23:1-4, 13-15

Friday
    You did not lie to us, but to God!   Acts 5: 1-5

Saturday
    Your sin is blotted out   Isaiah 6:1-7

Second Sunday in Lent   John 2:13-17
In the temple he found . . .

The Passover of the Jews was near, and Jesus went up to Jerusalem. In the temple he found people selling cattle, sheep, and doves, and the money-changers seated at their tables. Making a whip of cords, he drove all of them out of the temple, both the sheep and the cattle. He also poured out the coins of the money-changers and overturned their tables. He told those who were selling the doves, 'Take these things out of here! Stop making my Father's house a market-place!' His disciples remembered that it was written, 'Zeal for your house will consume me.'

This account of Jesus in the temple is recorded by John very near to the start of his Gospel, whereas Matthew, Mark and Luke place their reports in Holy Week itself. All agree that it was near the time of Passover, when the temple would be the focus of national activity with all who could manage the journey being there in Jerusalem to make their sacrifices. No doubt the money-changers were doing a roaring trade as they provided the temple currency needed to buy the necessary animals or birds. Anyone who has been to any event from a theatre production in the West End to a One-Day Cricket International in Grenada knows how galling it is to pay twice the price for a drink or an ice-cream because one is on the inside and has no alternative!

The temple in Jerusalem was, as we know, the focus for all Jewish worship. Its significance was far greater than any of our Christian buildings today, even our most awesome cathedrals or beloved local churches, for the temple replaced the Tabernacle of the Israelites wandering in the wilderness, and was regarded as the place where God dwelt, his earthly home. How then, we might wonder, had these inappropriate practices of trading and cheating been allowed to take place within the temple itself? We can only assume that with the insidious growth of materialism and decline of real spirituality, such behaviour was condoned, perhaps justified as 'defraying maintenance costs'!

The relationship between Jesus and the temple is fascinating. Looking back at his life through the events of Holy Week and Easter, we have no hesitation in believing that in Jesus himself was to be seen God's true earthly dwelling place. Jesus himself becomes the focus of God's presence amongst his people, as he implies later in the chapter (vv19-21). At this point, in what could be seen as a time of overlap between the old order and the new, Jesus comes to the temple. Here he might have expected to feel completely at home, totally at one with his Father in his Father's house. Indeed, Luke tells us (2:41-50) that in his last recorded visit there, as a boy of twelve, Jesus did feel this sense of being in his natural environment and was unwilling to leave its precincts. Now, at a crucial time, both in the celebration of the Jewish religion and in his own life, Jesus comes again to the temple. He comes, perhaps, to seek the fellowship and strength of God in the place which should have been the most tangible focus of his presence and nature. He comes, in the holiness of a life filled with God and empowered by the Holy Spirit, and instead encounters self-interest, deceit and exploitation; no wonder there is a violent reaction!

Moving on to the era in which we live, the era after Christ's death and resurrection, we hear Paul describing us, the Christian Church, as the new temple; 'Do you not know that you are God's temple and that God's Spirit dwells in you?' (1 Corinthians 3:16). As Jesus, by his Holy Spirit, seeks to move into more and more of our lives, both as individual Christians and as a Christian Church, what will he find? Can he dwell in our lives in peace and fellowship? What will he encounter in our hearts? Is some sort of breaking out inevitable?

Prayer:

Lord Jesus Christ, you who are God incarnate amongst us, you in whom the fullness of God was pleased to dwell, you have chosen to dwell in my life and in the life of your Church. Clear out what is rotten, selfish, corrupt and shameful, I pray, and may your zeal for God find an answering zeal within me.
Amen

Monday   Genesis 19:15-26
Flee for your life

When morning dawned, the angels urged Lot, saying, 'Get up, take your wife and your two daughters who are here, or else you will be consumed in the punishment of the city.' But he lingered; so the men seized him and his wife and his two daughters by the hand, the Lord being merciful to him, and they brought him out and left him outside the city. When they had brought them outside, they said, 'Flee for your life; do not look back or stop anywhere in the Plain; flee to the hills, or else you will be consumed.' . . . Then the Lord rained on Sodom and Gomorrah sulphur and fire from the Lord out of heaven; and he overthrew those cities, and all the Plain, and all the inhabitants of the cities, and what grew on the ground. But Lot's wife, behind him, looked back, and she became a pillar of salt.

The threat of imminent disaster often brings our true nature to light. In September 1995, St. Vincent was on 'hurricane watch' as Hurricane Marilyn sped westwards towards the little island. As the radio gave out its moment-by-moment reports of the whereabouts and strength of the storm, the residents of Chateaubelair battened down the hatches. Water containers were filled, stocks of food bought in, windows secured or boarded up, and many people took the time to check on elderly persons living alone – were their homes secure, did they have all they needed? Some, however, made no such preparations – as tensions rose and the skies darkened, a small group of young men chose to numb their senses with alcohol. From our balcony we observed them drinking themselves literally into the gutter. By the time the threat was over, the hurricane having turned further north, these men were insensible, beyond giving or receiving help!

The ancient tale of God's retribution against Sodom and Gomorrah is sandwiched in Genesis 19 between two stories of horrible depravity and shameful doings. Since the start of creation, God's light has been shining on his world, but at this time in history its beams illuminate the minds of only a few. Abraham has begun to understand something of the nature of the covenant God who made him and who is calling him to a life as the object and channel of great blessing. Even his closest associates, however, have hardly begun to grasp the message or accept the light. Abraham's nephew, Lot, having chosen the fertile plain of Jordan as his territory (Genesis 13:8f) has since discovered that wealth and ease can be the harbingers of sin and depravity; his life amongst the people of Sodom and Gomorrah has not been much fun! Now things have gone too far and God plans to destroy those evil cities, but, for the sake of Abraham, puts in place a plan to rescue Lot and his family. Even as they flee for their lives, Lot is bargaining with the angels and (in vv18-23, not printed above) makes a deal which will enable him to continue the life of a city-dweller, in the little city of Zoar! Their instructions are clear, they are to flee for their lives and not look back, but Lot's wife disobeys and becomes a pillar of salt.

Our minds, shaped as they are by over twenty centuries of Christian teaching and values, may find this sort of story hard to read and harder still to learn from. Whilst we may find some sort of justice in the punishment meted out to Sodom and Gomorrah (especially if we have read the earlier parts of this chapter!), perhaps we still feel that Lot's wife is treated harshly for what seems no more than a simple act of curiosity. Wouldn't any of us, in her shoes, have done the same? But maybe it was more than curiosity – Lot and his wife had been told to run for their lives, but did Lot's wife feel that what was important in her life was not ahead, but behind? Was her looking back symbolic of a desire to live her life in the old way, and an unwillingness to trust God and venture into the new? In this season of Lent are there aspects of our past life from which we need deliberately to turn away?

Prayer:

Holy God, your goodness is beyond my imagining; too often I fail to see how much my sin grieves you. I look at the depravity of the world around, but fail to notice my own inner acts of rebellion, my lack of trust in your will, which leads to disobedience. Have mercy upon me, I pray, as I turn my eyes and my will to your way. Amen

Tuesday

Exodus 32:7-10

An image of a calf

The Lord said to Moses, 'Go down at once! Your people, whom you brought up out of the land of Egypt, have acted perversely; they have been quick to turn aside from the way that I have commanded them; they have cast for themselves an image of a calf, and have worshipped it and sacrificed to it, and said, "These are your gods, O Israel, who brought you up out of the land of Egypt!" ' The Lord said to Moses, 'I have seen these people, how stiff-necked they are. Now let me alone, so that my wrath may burn hot against them and I may consume them; and of you I will make a great nation.'

The travels in the wilderness of the Israelite people under Moses' leadership were neither brief nor easy; for forty years they journeyed, meeting many difficulties on their way. Nor was this a time when the Israelites showed their absolute trust in God by their unshakeable joy and spirit of thankfulness! On the contrary, they lost no opportunity to grumble against their leadership – both human and divine – and to complain about hunger, thirst, enemy attack and each other! No wonder Moses spent so much time up the mountain with God! During one of these protracted absences – the forty days and nights in which Moses was given the ten commandments – the rebellion of the Israelites reached a climax. Under the direction of Aaron, no less, they cast a golden image of a calf and worship it, ascribing their salvation from slavery in Egypt to a mere idol.

For the most part, Christian preachers, leaders and writers today take pains to be faithful to the message of the New Testament. They warn their hearers and readers that the Christian path too is beset with difficulties and that in coming to Christ, one should not expect life to become problem-free. We have been warned . . . and yet, so often, when difficulties do arise in our lives we are taken by surprise and our faith is shaken. Not unlike our ancestors in the wilderness, we grumble and complain, we feel God has let us down and the minister becomes fair game!

Perhaps, again like the Israelites, we even go so far as to cast an idol – not a golden calf, we are far too sophisticated for that, but rather what I would like to call, 'the golden Christian'. We construct in our minds the image of the perfect Christian; one who attends all the right meetings and services, who cares for those around them, reads all the right books, is involved with any number of good causes and certainly never shouts at their children! This impossible standard then demands our worship and our sacrifice, as we weary ourselves with trying to live up to our own goals. We become convinced, as the subtle serpent works on our thinking, that it was by being this 'golden Christian' that we were saved at all, and that we must keep up the standards if we want to continue in God's favour. Yet this sort of attitude causes God sorrow, for it is not what he intends for those who tread the pilgrim way with him. All that God repeatedly asked for from the children of Israel was their love and their dependence; to recognise that they had not saved themselves, nor could they; nor can we, not by any amount of 'golden Christian' living.

Here, and in other parts of Exodus, Leviticus, Numbers and Deuteronomy, the rebellion has dire consequences; God's anger breaks out against his people and many lives are lost. Repeatedly Moses intercedes with God for the people, and the cycle of repentance-blessing-rebellion-punishment-repentance goes round again. Perhaps it is only as we study passages like these (try Numbers 16 as well!) and allow ourselves to see how our sin and rebellion angers God that we begin to realise how much Jesus has done for us in paying the price of our sin. As we look to him and him alone for salvation, our golden images of how we should live seem tawdry, and leave a bitter taste in our mouth, like the gold powder the Israelites were forced to drink (v20).

Prayer:

Lord God of my salvation, I confess that I have cast golden idols in my pilgrimage with you, I have trusted in my own strength to save me, and have disregarded what you have done for me in Jesus Christ. Give me grace today, I pray, to turn from these images to you and as I do so, to offer you my love and my total dependence. Amen

Wednesday   2 Samuel 6:1-11
The Lord burst forth

David again gathered all the chosen men of Israel, thirty thousand. David and all the people with him set out and went up Baale-judah, to bring up from there the ark of God, which is called by the name of the Lord of hosts who is enthroned on the cherubim. . . . When they came to the threshing-floor of Nacon, Uzzah reached out his hand to the ark of God and took hold of it, for the oxen shook it. The anger of the Lord was kindled against Uzzah; and God struck him there because he reached out his hand to the ark; and he died there beside the ark of God. David was angry because the Lord had burst forth with an outburst upon Uzzah; so that place is called Perez-uzzah to this day. David was afraid of the Lord that day; he said, 'How can the ark of the Lord come into my care?' So David was unwilling to take the ark of the Lord into his care in the city of David; instead David took it to the house of Obed-edom the Gittite. The ark of the Lord remained in the house of Obed-edom the Gittite for three months; and the Lord blessed Obed-edom and all his household.

In the modern world, and particularly in the so-called 'developed' countries, familiarity is the order of the day and even telephone sales persons use our Christian names as if they have known us all our lives. Returning to pastoral ministry in England after our years in the Caribbean, one of the things I have had to readjust to is hearing my husband called 'Andrew', rather than 'Rev'! I welcome that, of course. But, thinking of the way in which we treat God, I do wonder if we have lost something of the reverence for God which permeated earlier forms of worship and address. God is holy. Not just quite holy or even very holy, but Holy, Holy, Holy, as the Old Testament repeatedly says, using the most superlative form of the Hebrew language.

The history of the Ark of the Covenant makes fascinating reading, for back in Samuel's time we find it being used in battle almost as a talisman – a scheme which backfires disastrously on the Israelites (1 Samuel 4:1-11). After capture by the Philistines, however, it is clearly shown as a vessel of God's power, so much so that they return it to Israel, along with a guilt offering! Now, as it is being transported to Jerusalem, David's new capital city, we come across this, perhaps the 'worst' of all the stories of God's holiness breaking out against his people that we are looking at this week. It seems very unjust that Uzzah, who was only trying to help, should be killed for his pains.

Had King David himself forgotten the full extent of God's holiness? This story finds him bringing the ark back to Jerusalem with great rejoicing and celebration but is it possible to read between the lines a certain lack of reverence, even in David? The Ark of God was an extremely holy object and not something that could be used to bring good luck or blessing at will. As such it simply could not come into contact with sinful human flesh. God's total abhorrence of sin is a thread running throughout Scripture; God and sin cannot co-exist, something has to go. If we can begin to understand this, perhaps we would not ask of such a story, 'Why did this happen?' but would ask instead, 'Why did this not happen more often?' David is certainly shaken by this incident; he is angry against God for the death of Uzzah and then, we read, 'David was afraid of the Lord that day.' This fear leads him to send the ark elsewhere, until he hears how much blessing Obed-edom is receiving because of its presence (v12) and so he completes the task of bringing it to Jerusalem, again amidst much dancing and jubilation.

When we looked at the story of Mephibosheth last week, we rejected fear as a motive for our worship of God, but let us be careful not to treat this holy God as though he were little more than a good luck charm, whose blessing can be secured for our activities as and when we wish.

Prayer:

Like David, Lord, at times I am frightened by your holiness. At times I tremble, as I consider your hatred of sin, and I recognise how easily and how often I allow impure thoughts into my mind; untrue words into my mouth and unkind deeds into my life. Thank you for your ultimate sacrifice, the blood of Jesus which cleanses me from my sin. Amen

Thursday   Matthew 23:1-4, 13-15
Woe to you . . . hypocrites!

Then Jesus said to the crowds and to his disciples, 'The scribes and the Pharisees sit on Moses' seat; therefore, do whatever they teach you and follow it; but do not do as they do, for they do not practise what they teach. They tie up heavy burdens, hard to bear, and lay them on the shoulders of others; but they themselves are unwilling to lift a finger to move them. . . . But woe to you, scribes and Pharisees, hypocrites! For you lock people out of the kingdom of heaven. For you do not go in yourselves, and when others are going in, you stop them. Woe to you, scribes and Pharisees, hypocrites! For you cross sea and land to make a single convert, and you make the new convert twice as much a child of hell as yourselves.'

➢ These, along with the remaining verses of Matthew 23, form a scathing attack by Jesus on the hypocrisy of the religious leaders of his day. Seven times he repeats the phrase, 'Woe to you' and in v33 we read, 'You snakes, you brood of vipers! How can you escape being sentenced to hell?' Gentle Jesus, meek and mild?

➢ In C. S. Lewis' classic children's book, *The Lion, the Witch and the Wardrobe*, the four children hear talk of Aslan, a name which evokes different responses in all of them. After a while they learn that Aslan is not a man, as they had imagined, but a lion, and one of the children, Lucy, asks:

> 'Then he isn't safe?'
> 'Safe?' said Mr. Beaver, 'don't you hear what Mrs. Beaver tells you? Who said anything about safe? 'Course he isn't safe. But he's good.'

> On Radio Four recently, a vicar's wife who was told by a parishioner that she was rather frightening with her body-piercing and spiky hairstyle, replied, 'Good – Christianity is dangerous.'

Has Christianity become rather safe in our world today? In our efforts to be nice people, who respect and tolerate everybody and everything, have we lost the cutting edge of the gospel? Jesus preached a radical new lifestyle, and when some of those who had heard and followed him found the demands too great and turned away, he let them go. He didn't run after them to offer a diluted, easier-to-digest teaching in order to keep them with him (John 6:60-68).

Speaking out against what is wrong is rarely popular. After speaking on a radio broadcast in Grenada against domestic violence, Andrew was verbally abused by a small group of male prisoners on his next visit to the jail; 'So, Rev, you're with the women now – you're against us!' Our Methodist forefathers, the Tolpuddle Martyrs, had the courage to speak against the working conditions of their day and for the right to form a union, and suffered transportation to Australia as a punishment. We stand in a great tradition of men and women who, because of their faith in Christ, have not shunned confrontation with evil in society.

Before we take the moral high ground, however, and attack what is going on around us today, we need to realise that in these words Jesus was speaking to the established religious order of his day – a position held by the Christian Church in much of the world now. Jesus' strongest words of condemnation recorded in the gospels were not for 'sinners', be they prostitutes, thieves or cheats, but for religious people who, by their hypocrisy, prevented others from seeing and experiencing the grace of a loving God. As we lament the state of much of our Church today, can we recognise that we too may be part of the problem, guilty of keeping churches open but keeping them empty?

Prayer:

Lord Jesus Christ, these words of yours seem harsh; I want to turn away, or look over my shoulder and assume you are speaking to someone else. By the light of your Holy Spirit shining into my life, expose my hypocrisy and cleanse me, so that my actions may live up to my words and I may be a doorkeeper in your kingdom, guiding and welcoming others in. Amen

Friday   Acts 5:1-5
You did not lie to us, but to God!

But a man named Ananias, with the consent of his wife Sapphira, sold a piece of property; with his wife's knowledge, he kept back some of the proceeds, and brought only a part and laid it at the apostles' feet. 'Ananias,' Peter asked, 'why has Satan filled your heart to lie to the Holy Spirit and to keep back part of the proceeds of the land? While it remained unsold, did it not remain your own? And after it was sold, were not the proceeds at your disposal? How is it that you have contrived this deed in your heart? You did not lie to us, but to God!' Now when Ananias heard these words, he fell down and died. And great fear seized all who heard of it.

During my journey to an interview at Cambridge University for a place to study Theology, I skimmed through the famous and important book by Bishop John A. T. Robinson, *Honest to God*. An hour or so later, keen to impress my interviewers, (who included the well-known theologian Don Cupitt), when asked what book I had read most recently, I gave this title . . . I soon realised my mistake as I was closely questioned on a book I scarcely knew by people who knew it very well indeed. There is nothing like being caught out in a lie to make us feel wretched and humble!

Ananias (and later his wife, Sapphira – see vv7-11) must have thought their actions foolproof – they had agreed their story ahead of time; who was to know what price their land had fetched? They hadn't reckoned with the power of the Holy Spirit! Their act of deception ends dramatically and we are told again in v11 that 'great fear seized the whole church and all who heard of these things'. Once more, but now in the New Testament, we see God's anger breaking out at the sin of his people.

Any gardener knows that the worst sort of weed to have in a garden is the sort that puts out strong underground runners. Every visible sign of the weed may be dug up again and again, but while even so much as an inch or two of a runner remains in the soil, there is every likelihood of a new clump springing up somewhere else! Our human sin is not unlike these kinds of weed – there are manifestations of it on the surface of our lives which we cannot hide from our friends and family. We tell lies, and sometimes get found out; we cheat on our tax forms, and it is discovered by a vigilant clerk, we fall prey to lust or pride or back-biting or envy, or one of a multitude of faults, and those around us know it. We see our sin, we confess it and may seek to make what restitution we can. Believing in a forgiving God, we know ourselves to be absolved, and we hope that our problem is now dealt with.

What we may have ignored, however, are the running roots of our sinfulness, our rebellion against God's perfect will for our lives, which may be waiting to burst out elsewhere. These 'runners' are often attitudes, rather than actions, thoughts rather than words. What we have to realise is that it is not just the surface, visible sin which matters to a holy God, for he sees what goes on underneath as well. Peter points out to Ananias that he has lied to the Holy Spirit and sinned against God. We may recall the words of David in Psalm 51:4, 'Against you, you alone, have I sinned and done what is evil in your sight.' All sin is an outrage against God, whether it affects anyone else or not, whether it is even known by anyone else or not. Nowhere does Jesus say, 'Do your best, but don't worry if you can't make it', rather he says, 'Be perfect, therefore, as your heavenly Father is perfect' (Matthew 5:48). Lent is an appropriate season for some deep digging in the soil of our lives, as we face up to what we prefer to keep hidden. I wasn't offered a place at Cambridge, but I certainly learned something on the day of my interview about being 'Honest to God'!

Prayer:

Lord God, your standard of perfection seems out of my reach; as I examine my life I see so much which needs to be rooted out. I come to you as a patient to an expert surgeon – create in me a clean heart, and put a new and right spirit within me, I pray in Jesus' name. Amen

Saturday   Isaiah 6:1-7
Your sin is blotted out

In the year that King Uzziah died, I saw the Lord sitting on a throne, high and lofty; and the hem of his robe filled the temple. Seraphs were in attendance above him; each had six wings: with two they covered their faces, and with two they covered their feet, and with two they flew. And one called to another and said:

'Holy, holy, holy is the Lord of hosts;
the whole earth is full of his glory.'

The pivots on the thresholds shook at the voices of those who called, and the house filled with smoke. And I said: 'Woe is me! I am lost, for I am a man of unclean lips, and I live among a people of unclean lips; yet my eyes have seen the King, the Lord of hosts!' Then one of the seraphs flew to me, holding a live coal that had been taken from the altar with a pair of tongs. The seraph touched my mouth with it and said; 'Now that this has touched your lips, your guilt has departed and your sin is blotted out.'

Holy, holy, holy is the Lord of hosts . . .
Isaiah's ministry began with this dramatic revelation of God's utter holiness, which is totally pure and therefore, by necessity, totally separate from all that is unherolg. In worship and prayer today, let us too catch a glimpse of this holy Lord.

The whole earth is full of his glory . . .

This is God's world, and so it expresses, in a multitude of ways, something of his glory. Marvel today at the intricacy of a flower; stand amazed at the vastness of the night sky; consider how we ourselves are fearfully and wonderfully made.

Woe is me! I am lost, for I am a man of unclean lips . . .

Set against the holiness and glory of God, we too may feel lost. We know our lips are unclean – even today we may have spoken words that should have been left unsaid, or have failed to give that word of encouragement, or make that telephone call of comfort.

And I live among a people of unclean lips . . .

As well as my awareness of my own sin, I am sickened by the evil in the world – the news is full of violence, abuse, deceit, greed, self-seeking and corruption. I mourn for the sin of the world around me.

Yet my eyes have seen the King, the Lord of hosts!

Despite this desperate picture, of my sin and the world's sin, there is light and hope! There is a King on the throne of the universe and, in all my uncleanness, I have encountered him!

Now that this has touched your lips, your guilt has departed, and your sin is blotted out . . .

God himself has done what needs to be done – he has sent his messenger with a burning coal to cleanse me. From the fires of his own holiness, I receive holiness, a righteousness which does not come from obeying the law, but from faith in Christ Jesus, who has paid the price for my sin and presents me to God, washed clean and fit for service.

Questions:

1. Do you, on a daily basis, regard yourself as 'God's Temple' – the dwelling place of holy God? What might be the role of our house group or church fellowship in encouraging each other to think in this way?

2. Have you ever been aware of a tendency to be a 'Golden Christian; (see Tuesday). How can we stay rooted in the reality of God and not become swamped by our practice of religion?

3. What do you understand by holiness? Can you accept the idea that the holiness of God is a dangerous reality rather than a comforting concept?

4. Is 'sin' an out-dated religious word? Whom do we regard as sinners? What about ourselves?

Week 3: Fasting and Feasting

The first thing many of us may think of when we consider the demands of Lent is the idea of fasting. Many churches hold simple Lenten lunches during these six-and-a-half weeks, and even people who never come to church at all may well be familiar with the practice of 'giving something up for Lent'. The incarnation of Jesus demonstrates very clearly that, as Christians, we need to live a balanced life where body, soul and spirit are all attended to and all in balance. Fasting may well play a part in this; but so will feasting.

During this week, our Bible passages give us some insights into food, and our attitudes to it, as we try to learn from the experience of some Bible characters about saying 'yes' and saying 'no'.

Third Sunday in Lent   John 6:48-57
    Eat my flesh and drink my blood

Monday   Genesis 2:9, 15-17; 3:22-24
    'You may eat . . . you shall not eat'

Tuesday   1 Samuel 14:24-30
    How much better

Wednesday   2 Kings 7:3-9
    This is a day of good news

Thursday   Matthew 4:1-4
    He was famished

Friday   Mark 2:18-22
    And then they will fast

Saturday   Revelation 2:2-7
    I will give permission to eat from the tree of life

Third Sunday in Lent   John 6:48-57
Eat my flesh and drink my blood

'I am the bread of life. Your ancestors ate the manna in the wilderness, and they died. This is the bread that comes down from heaven, so that one may eat of it and not die. I am the living bread that came down from heaven. Whoever eats of this bread will live for ever; and the bread that I will give for the life of the world is my flesh.' The Jews then disputed among themselves, saying, 'How can this man give us his flesh to eat?' So Jesus said to them, 'Very truly, I tell you, unless you eat the flesh of the Son of Man and drink his blood, you have no life in you. Those who eat my flesh and drink my blood have eternal life, and I will raise them up on the last day; for my flesh is true food and my blood is true drink. Those who eat my flesh and drink my blood abide in me, and I in them. Just as the living Father sent me, and I live because of the Father, so whoever eats me will live because of me.'

Sundays, as mentioned before, are a celebration of the Resurrection and so they are always feast days – even during Lent. This may be very good news indeed to those of us who like our traditional Sunday lunches, Yorkshire puddings and all! This week we shall consider some of the biblical ideas about eating, and about not eating, and we start with this intense passage from John in which Jesus talks about himself as true food and true drink. John records that, on the previous day, Jesus attended to the physical hunger of crowds of his hearers, as he fed the five thousand with just five loaves and two fish. This action stirred up debate amongst the crowds, whom Jesus accuses of seeking him 'not because you saw signs, but because you ate your fill of the loaves' (6:26). Jesus saw the danger – as did many early Christian missionaries in various parts of the world who encountered 'rice Christians' – of people claiming conversion in order to gain materially. Human greed can always be exploited – in Chateaubelair we came across well-heeled missionaries, usually from smaller Christian denominations or sects based in rich countries, who offered presents to those who took new people along to their crusades. After Andrew had been invited to one such meeting three times in one morning, we discovered that the top prize (a photograph album) was on offer to anyone who took along a pastor from another church!

Therefore Jesus goes on to warn them, 'Do not work for the food that perishes, but for the food that endures for eternal life' (6:27). He does not want his followers to forget that physical food only sustains physical life and that will come to an end sooner or later for all of us. In order to receive the sort of life Jesus wants to give – eternal life – we need to eat and drink of his flesh and his blood.

Reading a passage like this we may not be at all surprised to know that cannibalism was among the many charges levelled against the early Christians during the days of persecution under hostile Roman emperors. Christians were believed to take part in strange rites involving the consumption of human flesh and blood. There has been a recent movement within parts of the Western Church to tone down the references to blood in our Communion liturgy and hymns.

There has been a recent movement within parts of the Western Church to tone down the references to blood in our Communion liturgy and hymns. Perhaps this reflects the paradox of a society which seems to crave murder, death, blood and gore on our TV screens, yet shrinks from confronting the real issues of death as they face and affect each of us. So we have had a big 'clean-up' operation, distancing ourselves from all that is offensive to our modern sensibilities. This even extends to the manner in which our food is sold – few of us today would want to try out a recipe which begins, 'First catch your rabbit . . .' as we are told our grandmothers would have had no qualms in doing!

In the Caribbean, (where a Christmas Eve tradition for our two sons was to watch a neighbour's pig being killed for the festivities!), we found no such squeamishness. No Good Friday service was complete without singing 'There is a fountain filled with blood, drawn from Immanuel's veins', a hymn no longer to be found in our hymn book. What we must keep in mind is the vital connection in the Jewish religion between blood and life. This is seen as early as Genesis (4:10), and becomes increasingly significant under Moses (Leviticus 17:11). Jesus is inviting us not merely to follow his example or obey his teaching, but to partake of his very life.

Prayer:

Lord Jesus, in the midst of so much plenty, so much waste, so much excess, I know that I have often been content with a spiritual starvation diet. I have only picked and nibbled at all that you want to feed me – your own self. Spread your feast for me this Lent, I pray, and give me grace to partake with joy and thanksgiving. Amen

Monday   Genesis 2:9, 15-17; 3:22-24
'You may eat . . . you shall not eat'

Out of the ground, the Lord God made to grow every tree that is pleasant to the sight and good for food, the tree of life also in the midst of the garden, and the tree of the knowledge of good and evil. . . . The Lord God took the man and put him in the garden of Eden to till it and keep it. And the Lord God commanded the man, 'You may eat freely of every tree of the garden; but of the tree of the knowledge of good and evil you shall not eat, for in the day that you eat of it you shall die.'

Then the Lord God said, 'See, the man has become like one of us, knowing good and evil; and now, he might reach out his hand and take also from the tree of life, and eat, and live forever' – therefore the Lord God sent him forth from the garden of Eden, to till the ground from which he was taken. He drove out the man; and at the east of the garden of Eden he placed the cherubim, and a sword flaming and turning to guard the way to the tree of life.

At present, we live in a culture which is confused in its attitude to food. More varieties of food are sold in our supermarkets than ever before. New restaurants and eating places abound. Food-and-drink TV programmes are popular viewing and their presenters are numbered among our modern gurus – one even has the distinction of being included in the dictionary! On the other hand (perhaps in consequence) diet and fitness classes are also springing up everywhere, and refusing puddings, resisting chocolate or giving up biscuits is seen as 'being good'. Issues of food safety are frequently in the news, many of them caused or exacerbated by the consumer's continual demand for cheaper and cheaper food. Surveys suggest that to most people in the UK, the price of food is more important than its quality or safety. We are left unsure about whether food is good or bad for us.

In these ancient verses from Genesis we find God both providing and prohibiting food. The garden of Eden which he has created for humankind to live in, is full of 'every tree that is pleasant to the sight and good for food'. As we consider the enormous variety of tastes and textures which God has created for our enjoyment, we must come to the conclusion that God is in favour of eating and enjoying it! Living in the Caribbean introduced us to a whole new range of delicious flavours – mangoes straight from the tree, soursop made into a refreshing drink, juicy sappodillas, breadfruit roasted on a coal-pot in our yard. Jesus too is clearly not anti-food; he provides food generously for those in need, as we considered yesterday; he attends meals, parties and celebrations, suggesting that he was not ascetic in his own lifestyle.

There is one food, however, that is not permitted for Adam and Eve, one tree from which they are forbidden to eat: the tree of the knowledge of good and evil. Surely, with so much good fruit around to satisfy their needs and desires, there would be no danger of Adam or Eve disobeying? Yet we know what happened. Tempted by the serpent, Eve saw that the tree 'was good for food and that it was a delight to the eyes, and that the tree was to be desired to make one wise' (3:6) so she succumbed. Wouldn't any one of us have done the same? When faced with temptation we too are weak, the lust of our eyes leads us on and we, like Eve, go too far. With us it may be a weakness for clothes, or jewellery, or hi-tech gadgets. It may, indeed, be food itself, for the doctors tell us that many of the health problems of the 'developed' world are related to over-eating – surely an outrage in a world of so much hunger and starvation. I believe that we can take from this well-known Bible passage the message that God has provided a good world for us to enjoy, but that there are times when we should say no.

Prayer:

Lord God, living in this 'shopping culture' of the twenty-first century, it is sometimes so hard to say no. Like Eve, I see things that are good and delightful, and I want them, regardless of the cost. May the sword of your Spirit flaming and turning in my life guard my way and give me such wisdom as I need to live as you would have me live today. Amen

Tuesday
1 Samuel 14:24-30
How much better

Now Saul committed a very rash act on that day. He had laid an oath on the troops, saying, 'Cursed be anyone who eats food before it is evening and I have been avenged on my enemies.' So none of the troops tasted food. All the troops came upon a honeycomb; and there was honey on the ground. When the troops came upon the honeycomb, the honey was dripping out; but they did not put their hands to their mouths, for they feared the oath. But Jonathan had not heard his father charge the troops with the oath; so he extended the staff that was in his hand, and dipped the tip of it in the honeycomb, and put his hand to his mouth; and his eyes brightened. Then one of the soldiers said, 'Your father strictly charged the troops with an oath, saying, "Cursed be anyone who eats food this day." And so the troops are faint.' Then Jonathan said, 'My father has troubled the land; see how my eyes have brightened because I have tasted a little of this honey. How much better if today the troops had eaten freely of the spoil taken from their enemies; for now the slaughter among the Philistines has not been great.'

Studying the life of King Saul, one might feel tempted to sub-title his reign, '101 ways of getting it wrong'! A man with so much potential, but whose life goes from bad to worse as he is consumed by fear, jealousy, paranoia and lack of spiritual understanding. In the previous chapter he has angered Samuel by offering sacrifices to God, something which, not being a priest, he had no authority to do. In the next chapter he thinks he knows better than the instructions given to him by God and incurs Samuel's wrath again. Here he calls his troops to a fast as they follow Jonathan's surprise attack on the Philistines to finish off the battle. Fasting is a normal religious rite in the Old Testament, sometimes expressing penitence, humility or grief, sometimes to secure the guidance and help of God. However, we are led to understand, by the comment of the writer and also by Jonathan's later remarks, that fasting as a preparation for battle is not a good idea. Inevitably the troops are weakened by their abstention from food and the victory they achieve is not as great as it might have been. Indeed, their fast leads them into further sin, for when they are again permitted to eat, they fall on the spoil of their enemies with such ravenous hunger that they eat the animals with the blood still in them (vv31-33).

The vow having been made, of course, has to stand, and later in the chapter, when God will not answer Saul at all, he realises that there has been sin in the camp. By the process of 'Urim and Thummim', an ancient method of divining God's mind, probably through the use of stones, Saul finds that Jonathan is the cause of the sin. Jonathan himself confesses that he ate some honey and offers to die, but the people will not permit this. Jonathan has been the prime mover in this glorious victory against the Philistines and so, as the writer puts it, 'the people ransomed Jonathan and he did not die' (v45).

Perhaps Saul's fundamental mistake was to believe that he could somehow twist the arm of God by his piety. If so, he is not so very different from some of us today, and we can all learn from his failures. God has, in his goodness, given us many 'means of grace' by which we can draw closer to him. Fasting is one such way, so is prayer, Bible study, participation in public worship, sharing in the Lord's Supper, other acts of self-denial and generosity to others. However, if we try to use these methods not, as they were intended, as a loving response to God's love for us, but rather to try to gain God's favour and enlist his support for our plans, they will not work. Worse than that, they may cause disaster. There is a place for piety and discipline in our Christian lives, as we are examining as we go through Lent, but Saul shows us the dangers of living by ritual, rather than by spiritual reality.

Prayer:

Lord God, I recognise today how often I have misunderstood your amazing parent-love for me. I realise how childish I have been in my response to you. Forgive me for those times when I have tried to earn your favour, or persuade you by my actions. Thank you for your grace, which is ever new, raising me up as I offer myself to you once more. Amen

Wednesday   2 Kings 7:3-9
This is a day of good news

Now there were four leprous men outside the city gate, who said to one another, 'Why should we sit here until we die? If we say, "Let us enter the city", the famine is in the city, and we shall die there; but if we sit here, we shall also die. Therefore, let us desert to the Aramean camp; if they spare our lives, we shall live; and if they kill us, we shall but die.' So they arose at twilight to go to the Aramean camp; but when they came to the edge of the Aramean camp, there was no one there at all. . . . When these leprous men had come to the edge of the camp, they went into a tent, ate and drank, carried off silver, gold, and clothing, and went and hid them. Then they came back, entered another tent, carried off things from it, and went and hid them. Then they said to one another, 'What we are doing is wrong. This is a day of good news; if we are silent and wait until morning light, we will be found guilty; therefore let us go and tell the king's household.'

Living back in Britain, having people for a meal or friends to stay is relatively straightforward – I decide what we are going to have to eat, and shop accordingly. In St. Vincent, I had to learn to do things the other way round. The local shops were limited in what they stocked and Chateaubelair was over an hour's car journey from the capital, Kingstown, the only shopping centre of any size on the island. Also, I never knew what food might arrive at the manse during the day. On many a Monday morning, as I began the washing, a bucket of freshly caught jackfish would be presented to me at the door – often needing gutting immediately! Throughout our time in the Caribbean, people were so generous with gifts of fruit, vegetables, fish and meat that our menus had to be planned around whatever needed eating up first! On one occasion I did want to do a particular recipe for a particular guest and needed a 'water nut' – a coconut fresh from the tree, still green and full of liquid. I asked a friend to ask around and see if she could find one for me, and within an hour more than a dozen water nuts were brought to the manse!

Of course, I would not want to suggest that the Methodist people of Britain are not equally generous. After telling the story at a Network meeting of a retired nurse in Chateaubelair who had brought half of her prize catch, a red snapper, to our gate because she knew we had visitors, an elderly lady here in Stoke-on-Trent presented me with a bunch of bananas after Sunday morning service; 'I haven't grown them,' she said, 'they're from Tesco, but they are Caribbean!' What a blessing such givers are to those around them.

The four men in our story begin with a fairly hopeless outlook on life – their land of Samaria is being besieged, food is so scarce that people are paying high prices for such cuts as a donkey's head, and it seems that whatever they do, they will die. So they decide to venture into the enemy camp, where perhaps mercy might be shown to them. What a surprise awaits them – God has frightened away the Aramean army and the camp is deserted. They soon find as much food and drink as they can consume and, when they have eaten and drunk their fill, gold, silver and clothing up for grabs! After making free with their loot for a while, however, they stop and think and their words should be our motto in the Christian Church: 'This is a day of good news!' They return to their own city and send word to the king and, in time, all can share in the bounty.

Evangelism has often been described as 'one hungry beggar showing another where to find bread' – as we feast at the Lord's table, do we not long to invite others to be there too?

Prayer:

Thank you, Lord, that you have invited me to your feast. Thank you for all the riches of Christ that you have made available to me. Give me that love and generosity of spirit which wants to share what you have done and who you are with all I meet. In Jesus' name. Amen

Thursday   Matthew 4:1-4
He was famished

Then Jesus was led up by the Spirit into the wilderness to be tempted by the devil. He fasted forty days and forty nights, and afterwards he was famished. The tempter came and said to him, 'If you are the Son of God, command these stones to become loaves of bread.' But he answered, 'It is written,

> **"One does not live by bread alone,**
> **but by every word that comes from**
> **the mouth of God." '**

Matthew is wonderfully down-to-earth in his report of Jesus fasting in the wilderness. After forty days without food, he says, Jesus 'was famished'. I'm sure we all would have been. I have never experienced that kind of hunger, and I doubt that many of us have. During our time in the Caribbean, particularly in the little rural town of Chateaubelair, we lived among many very poor people, but St. Vincent is a blessedly fertile island – it was said that in one particularly fertile valley, known locally as Mesopotamia, an umbrella pushed into the ground would grow! Almost everyone owned some land, on which they grew fruit and vegetables, generally including 'pigeon peas', a small pulse which grew on a large bush and supplied many people with a rich source of vegetable protein.   So hunger was rare, and starvation unheard of – sadly, this is far from the case in many regions.

It is to the shame of the 'developed' countries that despite all the advances of science and agriculture, which produce bigger and better crops, we still have not been able to 'feed the world'. When we, regarding ourselves as civilised, Christian societies, react in horror at tales of institutionalised violence or other ritual practices among some races and peoples, perhaps we should ask ourselves searching questions about the selfishness and greed which go unquestioned in the way life is lived in much of the 'West'. I have observed a rising trend in advertising in

Britain which preaches the message 'Some things are too good to share'.

My first attempts at fasting came in my university days, when twenty-four hour fasts for Oxfam were organised from time to time, and Christian Union leaders were expected to join in! Around the same time, I discovered by chance that a fellow-student I knew only a little had joined with her sister in pledging to miss lunch every Thursday, as they prayed that their mother would come to faith in Christ. There was something about this quiet, almost secretive, self-denial which challenged me and which, to me, still brings into focus much of the point of fasting as Christians today. When linked with prayer, fasting is a way of saying to God that we are deeply concerned about the situations for which we pray; that we earnestly want to see change, and that we are willing to go without some of the comforts of our own lives as a pledge of our commitment. There is not space here for a full discussion of fasting, and there are many good Christian books available dealing with this subject. However, it is certainly true that the frequent internal rumblings and hunger pangs experienced on a fast day can serve as reminders to pray, and that without regular heavy meals, I am less likely to doze off over my prayers!

It comes as no surprise that after a forty-day fast, the devil should try to tempt Jesus with food. Why not turn a few stones into loaves of bread? Bread is good – we know that Jesus shared in and even provided bread on many occasions, why not here? On Monday, when we considered Adam and Eve, we noted that, whilst food, like much in life, is good, there are times to say yes and times to say no. Eve failed to make the distinction; Jesus does not. He is not looking for a way to gratify his own desires, but is in training for a life of perfect obedience, a life lived according to every word of God. What about us – have we yet realised that 'more is not always better'?

Prayer:

Thank you, Lord, that you have provided me with so much good food; potatoes or breadfruit, strawberries or mangoes, sausages or saltfish – so much to delight me. Thank you, too, that you have created me with the ability to make choices, to say yes and to say no. Help me to learn how to use all these good gifts to your glory.
Amen

Friday   Mark 2:18-22
And then they will fast

Now John's disciples and the Pharisees were fasting; and people came and said to him, 'Why do John's disciples and the disciples of the Pharisees fast, but your disciples do not fast?' Jesus said to them, 'The wedding-guests cannot fast while the bridegroom is with them, can they? As long as they have the bridegroom with them they cannot fast. The days will come when the bridegroom is taken away from them, and then they will fast on that day.

'No one sews a piece of unshrunk cloth on an old cloak; otherwise, the patch pulls away from it, the new from the old, and a worse tear is made. And no one puts new wine into old wineskins; otherwise, the wine will burst the skins, and the wine is lost, and so are the skins; but one puts new wine into fresh wineskins.'

The first time we joined West Indian friends for a beach picnic, we had a bit of a surprise. In true English style we packed up our cool box with sandwiches, cakes and cold drinks, but, when others arrived with their goodies our fare was regarded as no more than a snack! Children arrived with armfuls of sticks, young people balancing huge aluminium pots of water on their heads, women with their baskets of fruit and vegetables, men with their fishing knives and spears! Much of this had been carried a considerable distance from the nearest road, but was deemed essential for a proper picnic. Fires were lit, breadfruit roasted, coconuts grated to make dumplings, vegetables boiled, fresh fish caught in the sea and slowly the appetising smell of fish broth wafted across the beach – no fast food this! Needless to say, our generous friends did not expect us to sit by with our 'snack' and watch them tuck into their feast – there was more than enough for all to share.

Again in this passage, Jesus tells us that there are times to eat and times not to eat. His words link the practice of fasting with times of unfulfilment, times of seeking and concern; fasting is a response to an acknowledged need. This same understanding was shown long before by King David. After the child born to him by Bathsheba becomes sick, he fasts and pleads with God for the life of the child. When the child dies, his aides are concerned that he may be so upset as to harm himself, but instead he rises, washes and eats. In response to his puzzled servants he replies, 'While the child was still alive, I fasted and wept; for I said, "Who knows? The Lord may be gracious to me, and the child may live." But now he is dead; why should I fast? Can I bring him back again? I shall go to him, but he will not return to me.' (2 Samuel 12:22-23). We too need to recognise that the times in which we live are times of need, of longing, of unfulfilment and we need to pray, 'Your Kingdom come.'

The three short years Jesus lived among his disciples, preaching, healing and even raising the dead, were years of fulfilment, years of celebration, years of feasting, but Jesus knew this would not last. He warns that the bridegroom will soon be taken away, then the time for fasting will come. He goes on to give two illustrations to do with mixing the old and the new – to his hearers it would have been obvious that new wine could not be stored in old wineskins, and that unshrunk cloth could not patch an old cloak – perhaps in our pre-packaged, disposable culture we have lost sight of some of this knowledge. Jesus draws a clear distinction between the old order, now coming to an end, and the new order he is inaugurating. We can apply this truth to our lives. For each one of us, as we come to Christ, a new order begins – many of the structures and trappings of our old lives will no longer be appropriate for the radically new lifestyle to which Christ calls us. A lifestyle in which we may even have to examine what we eat, and how much!

Prayer:

Lord God, as I look around your world, and as I look at my life, I see great need. I know that there is much work you want to do in me and through me, and I pledge myself to be open to your Spirit leading me in prayer and in action that your Kingdom may be fulfilled in my life and in your world. In Jesus' name. Amen

Saturday   Revelation 2:2-7
I will give permission to eat from the tree of life

'I know your works, your toil and your patient endurance.
I know that you cannot tolerate evildoers; you have tested
those who claim to be apostles but are not, and have found
them to be false. I also know that you are enduring
patiently and bearing up for the sake of my name, and that
you have not grown weary. But I have this against you,
that you have abandoned the love that you had at first.
Remember then from what you have fallen; repent, and do
the works you did at first. If not, I will come to you and
remove your lampstand from its place, unless you repent.
Yet this is to your credit: you hate the works of the
Nicolaitans, which I also hate. Let anyone who has an ear
listen to what the Spirit is saying to the churches. To
everyone who conquers, I will give permission to eat from
the tree of life that is in the paradise of God.'

➢ At the end of a week spent considering our eating habits,
   both physically and spiritually, we look today at one of the
   seven letters to the churches recorded in Revelation 2
   and 3.

➢ It may seem to bear little relation to our theme of 'Fasting
   and Feasting' until we come to the very last line. Here, the
   punishment of Genesis 2, which we looked at on Monday, is
   reversed; permission to eat from the tree of life is given – the
   wheel of Scripture has come full circle.

I know your works, your toil and your patient endurance. . . . I also know that you are enduring patiently and bearing up for the sake of my name, and that you have not grown weary.

These are wonderful words of encouragement to a church suffering from persecution. Do they speak to us in our situation today, wherever we live, whatever the state of our local congregation may be? We are assured by Jesus' words that he is not unaware of what we do in his name. Perhaps you are feeling tired; tired of church, tired of fund-raising and committee-going, tired of going against the grain in a secular world, tired of trying . . . Let these words speak to you and lift you today – Jesus sees, Jesus knows; it is not for the sake of those who seem to be ungrateful or worse that you are patiently enduring, it is for the sake of his name.

But I have this against you, that you have abandoned the love that you had at first.

Once again, love surfaces in Jesus' words to his Church. Love is the supreme requirement of God from his people. Any service, not given in love, is not primarily what God is asking for. Just as, for most of us, our initial response to God was a response of love, let us seek and pray to recapture that in our relationship with him now.

To everyone who conquers, I will give permission to eat from the tree of life that is in the paradise of God.

When Adam and Eve sinned in eating of the tree of the knowledge of good and evil, God did not want them to compound the disaster by eating of the tree of life and so remaining eternally in their sin. The tree of life had to be guarded and prohibited, until when? Until Adam and Eve's descendants had learned a new way to live; had the law written upon their hearts, through the new covenant made in the blood of Jesus. Until those who follow Christ in every land and in every circumstance had learned to overcome, to conquer, not in their own strength, but in the name of Jesus and in his name alone. To those – to us – God has given permission to eat from the tree of life that is in the paradise of God. Thanks be to God!

Questions:

1. There are sincere believers today who are asking, 'Why so much blood in the Christian gospel?' Is it possible to have Christianity without emphasis on the blood of Christ?

2. 'Just say no' is a message being given to young people today with regard to taking illegal drugs. As Christians may not wish to suggest that Christianity is repressive, but do we *all* need to learn that there are times to 'just say no'?

3. Self-denial is not supposed to be a means of 'twisting God's arm'. Have you ever found yourself using it in this way? Can you, your house group, or your church testify to the power of prayer, fasting or other forms of self-denial?

Week 4: Rejection

The climax of this week's readings comes on Saturday as we meditate on the famous words from Isaiah: 'He was despised and rejected.' From Genesis to Revelation the Bible is full of stories about rejection, and the theme of humanity's rejection of God is a vital strand of the story of the Scriptures. During this week, we shall look at various aspects of rejection; the rejection of God and of his people by a rebellious world; our own rejection of God and, in one case, his rejection of us. This may not make for uplifting reading, but rejection is a part of life and a significant factor in Jesus' journey to the cross. We share that journey as we examine our own reasons for, and reactions to, rejection.

Fourth Sunday in Lent   John 10:24-39
    'It is not for a good work . . . but for blasphemy'

Monday   1 Samuel 8:4-20
    'They have not rejected you,
    but they have rejected me'

Tuesday   1 Samuel 15:10-31
    The Lord has rejected you

Wednesday   Mark 6:1-6
    He could do no deed of power there

Thursday   Mark 10:17-22
    He went away grieving

Friday   Mark 15:6-15
    Release Barabbas instead

Saturday   Isaiah 53:3-8
    Rejected by others

Fourth Sunday in Lent   John 10:24-39
'It is not for a good work . . . but for blasphemy'

So the Jews gathered around him and said to him, 'How long will you keep us in suspense? If you are the Messiah, tell us plainly.' Jesus answered, 'I have told you, and you do not believe. The works that I do in my Father's name testify to me; but you do not believe, because you do not belong to my sheep . . . The Father and I are one.' The Jews took up stones again to stone him. Jesus replied, 'I have shown you many good works from the Father. For which of these are you going to stone me?' The Jews answered, 'It is not for a good work that we are going to stone you, but for blasphemy, because you, though only a human being, are making yourself God.' Jesus answered, '. . . If I am not doing the works of my Father, then do not believe me. But if I do them, even though you do not believe me, believe the works, so that you may know and understand that the Father is in me and I am in the Father.' Then they tried to arrest him again, but he escaped from their hands.

Jesus did not experience universal popularity in his lifetime, nor has he since. It is not true to say that all who met him loved him, nor that he was able to win everyone over to himself. All four Gospel writers present a picture of conflict with the Jewish authorities, of opposition to his teaching and, ultimately, of hostile plots to bring about his death. John, in particular, records many tense confrontations between Jesus and the Jews, such as the one in today's reading. We see a Jewish hierarchy not simply indifferent to Jesus, but actively rejecting him.

The Church of Jesus Christ has also known opposition, hostility and rejection. From the early days of blood-curdling persecution under a series of Roman Emperors to the oppression and even torture of Christians in some countries in the twenty-first century, the Church too has seldom, if ever, experienced universal popularity.

Why is this so? How can a person, or a movement, whose central teaching is that God loves us and that we should love one another, possibly generate so much hatred? Is it a measure of how far the human race has fallen that, although we have been made in the image of a holy God, at times our sinful nature reacts violently against purity? Perhaps in a way, this is the natural consequence of week three's theme – that holiness and sin cannot co-exist. In recent weeks I have heard of a child at school who refuses to swear finding himself surrounded by a gang trying to force him to do so; of a minister who offers friendly words to boys who are trying to intimidate her being jeered at and victimised; of a schoolteacher who stands apart from the negative, destructive talk of the staff room being ostracised by her colleagues. Plato, living four centuries before Christ, once said that if ever it should happen that a perfectly pure, totally good man should walk the earth, then human beings would kill him. So perhaps we should not be surprised to be a minority, nor should we be unduly upset when our message is not well-received or given the kind of media coverage we might like. (Although it has to be said that much of the bad press given to the Church is, sadly, deserved.)

How do we respond to this rejection? How did Jesus respond? What strikes me about this and similar passages, is that Jesus' opponents are not willing to believe the evidence of their eyes. Several times Jesus calls on them to 'believe the works' yet, although they virtually admit that his works are good, they will not see them as signs of his divine nature and authority. The Church, too, may be tempted to say, 'believe the works', calling on the world to notice that over the centuries, Christians have been at the forefront of education and health care, of social transformation and human rights campaigning. I heard recently that a survey has shown that the vast majority of people involved in voluntary charity work in the UK are church members.

But is there any point in saying this? If the works of Jesus himself did not deter his opposition, why should ours? I believe that we have to face up to the truth that to many people the gospel itself is offensive. It is not what we do (although, of course, our works must always be good, just as Jesus' were) but what we believe that causes people to reject Christianity.

Prayer:

Lord God, in the face of rejection I want to defend myself and defend you. Help me, like Paul, to know nothing except Jesus Christ, and him crucified, even when that is a stumbling-block to my colleagues and foolishness to my family. Amen

Monday   1 Samuel 8:4-20
'They have not rejected you, but they have rejected me'

Then all the elders of Israel gathered together and came to Samuel at Ramah, and said to him, 'You are old and your sons do not follow in your ways; appoint for us, then, a king to govern us, like other nations.' But the thing displeased Samuel when they said, 'Give us a king to govern us.' Samuel prayed to the Lord, and the Lord said to Samuel, 'Listen to the voice of the people in all that they say to you; for they have not rejected you, but they have rejected me from being king over them. Just as they have done to me, from the day I brought them up out of Egypt to this day, forsaking me and serving other gods, so also they are doing to you. Now then, listen to their voice; only – you shall solemnly warn them, and show them the ways of the king who shall reign over them.' . . . But the people refused to listen to the voice of Samuel; they said, 'No! but we are determined to have a king over us, so that we also may be like other nations, and that our king may govern us and go out before us and fight our battles.'

Clearing goods through customs in St. Vincent was always a long process, and never Andrew's favourite task. On one occasion, however, as we drove towards the gates of the dockyards, we were amazed to see them being hastily opened by a deferential official. As we swept through, wondering if Andrew's ministry had borne surprise fruit among the dockers, we heard the man mutter, 'Good morning, Mr. Mitchell.' That explained everything. In the dazzle of a Caribbean day, behind tinted glass, Andrew had been mistaken for the Prime Minister, to whom he bore a passing resemblance. They were not welcoming us at all, but Dr. James Mitchell.

That particular mistake never occurred again, but generally, I have found that being married to a Methodist minister (particularly in the Caribbean) has gained me access which may otherwise have been unavailable. Just occasionally, however, the reverse has been true – as it has been discovered that I, to some extent, represent Andrew, or Methodism, or Christianity, doors have been closed and friendliness withdrawn. Whatever kind of rejection we experience, it always hurts.

As the last of the judges, Samuel had been ruling Israel, under the guidance of God. When the Israelites asked for a king, Samuel was hurt – it could only mean that they no longer wanted his style of leadership. Displeased, he prays to God, who comforts him, '. . . they have not rejected you, but they have rejected me from being king over them.' The God of Israel is no stranger to rejection, as the whole story of the Old Testament demonstrates. Yesterday we considered how that rejection continued into the life and ministry of Jesus and of the Christian Church, concluding, rather bleakly, that the gospel inevitably provokes a degree of rejection.

Perhaps we have all known this rejection of Christianity as we have invited neighbours to a church service and watched their eyes become guarded as they hastily make their excuses. Maybe, because of our convictions, we have gone from door to door, collecting for Christian Aid and been met with rudeness, or stood in a shopping precinct, shaking a tin and wondering if we really have become invisible! Perhaps the rejections we have experienced because of our faith have gone deeper. Many young people fear that to refuse to have sex before marriage because of their Christian beliefs will jeopardise their relationships and bring about rejection. Holding out for absolute honesty in business dealings may mean rejection by colleagues. I recall a co-student on Teaching Practice in a big comprehensive school who, because of her Christian principles, refused to use illegally photocopied material, and suffered mockery and verbal abuse from members of staff as a result.

To all who have known rejection because of their faith, God speaks again the words he spoke to Samuel, '. . . they have not rejected you but they have rejected me.' God's kingly rule over hearts and lives will, more often than not, produce a counter-reaction of rebellion. When, by our lives or our words, we challenge this state of rebellion against God in those around us, rejection may well follow. God knows and understands. God has been there before us and stands beside us.

Prayer:

> Lord Jesus, you who said, 'Blessed are those who are persecuted for righteousness' sake, for theirs is the kingdom of heaven', thank you that as I try to stand up for you, you stand beside me. Amen

Tuesday
1 Samuel 15:10-31
The Lord has rejected you

The word of the Lord came to Samuel: 'I regret that I made Saul king, for he has turned back from following me, and has not carried out my commands.' . . . Then Samuel said to Saul, 'Stop! I will tell you what the Lord said to me last night.' He replied, 'Speak.' Samuel said, 'Though you are little in your own eyes, are you not the head of the tribes of Israel? The Lord anointed you king over Israel. And the Lord sent you on a mission, and said, "Go, utterly destroy the sinners, the Amalekites, and fight against them until they are consumed." Why then did you not obey the voice of the Lord? Why did you swoop down on the spoil and do what was evil in the sight of the Lord?' . . . Saul said to Samuel, 'I have sinned; for I have transgressed the commandment of the Lord and your words, because I feared the people and obeyed their voice. Now therefore, I pray, pardon my sin, and return with me, so that I may worship the Lord.' Samuel said to Saul, 'I will not return with you; for you have rejected the word of the Lord, and the Lord has rejected you from being king over Israel.'

Rejection is damaging. When parents continually reject their children by failing to notice and praise their successes, but see only their faults, lives are scarred. When children repeatedly reject the counsel and concern of their parents, breakdown takes place. When partners within a marriage reject each other on whatever level, deep wounds are caused. As we consider our relationship with God, again there is rejection, as Saul's life illustrates.

Here, only seven chapters after yesterday's reading when God gave Samuel the go-ahead to appoint a king over Israel, we find that things are starting to go wrong and even that God is having regrets! If possible, read the whole of chapter 15 to get the full story of Saul's disobedience and God's subsequent rejection of him as king. Briefly, it had been Saul's specific commission to destroy the Amalekites, a group of people who had incurred God's wrath years before by opposing the Israelites in the wilderness. After a successful battle against them, however, Saul bows to the pressure of his army and, instead of utterly destroying God's enemies, he allows them to keep some of the spoil, and he also keeps alive the king, Agag. We have observed before that Saul always seems to get it wrong; here he makes the basic mistake of thinking he knows better than God. His actions may seem reasonable, even humane, but they go against God's clear instructions to him.

We can sympathise with Saul, for, like Job, most of us have, at times, questioned God. Why does God allow certain things to go unpunished? Does Jesus really mean that we should turn the other cheek? Why does the New Testament speak out so uncompromisingly on sexual immorality? We may feel that biblical principles cannot possibly make sense in twenty-first century life, and so we consider ourselves free to reinterpret traditional teachings, to concoct a more 'sophisticated' theology. Beware! We are on dangerous ground. Of course the message of the Bible and the teachings of Christ have to be examined in the light of every new age and culture, but always within the limitations fixed by a spirit of obedience to God.

Although Saul continues as king for a while after this incident, his life deteriorates, and it is almost a question of marking time until David, the 'man after [God's own] heart' (Acts 13:22) can take over. Samuel tells Saul very clearly that God has now rejected him as king. We may find this idea rather difficult to accept; we are quite at home with the idea of humanity rejecting God, but we don't like to think of God rejecting us. But this is not the only time in the Bible that this happens; the Exile is seen as God's rejection of Israel (2 Kings 17:20 and in Jeremiah) and in Romans, Paul writes at length of the way in which God 'gave up' or 'handed over' those who were persistently disobedient to him (Romans 1:18-32). As we struggle to understand more of the nature of God, we have to hold in one hand the truth that God is love, that God is full of compassion and grace, that God is longing to forgive and restore and reconcile every part of his creation, yet in the other hand we must also seek to grasp the reality of a God who is angered by our continual disobedience, who sees our internal rebellion against his will, and who – if we persist in rejecting him and going our own way – will never force us but may ultimately leave us to our own devices. We have been warned!

Prayer:

Lord God, like the father of the prodigal son, you have been hurt by my rejection, yet you are watching out for my return to you, stretching out arms of love and speaking words of restoration. Thank you, Lord. Amen

Wednesday   Mark 6:1-6
He could do no deed of power there

He left that place and came to his home town, and his disciples followed him. On the sabbath he began to teach in the synagogue, and many who heard him were astounded. They said, 'Where did this man get all this? What is this wisdom that has been given to him? What deeds of power are being done by his hands! Is not this the carpenter, the son of Mary and brother of James and Joses and Judas and Simon, and are not his sisters here with us?' And they took offence at him. Then Jesus said to them, 'Prophets are not without honour, except in their home town, and among their own kin, and in their own house.' And he could do no deed of power there, except that he laid his hands on a few sick people and cured them. And he was amazed at their unbelief.

I was born and brought up on the outskirts of Wolverhampton, but, after marriage, moved to live in Richmond, Swaledale. When, after a few years there, Andrew applied for and was offered a job in a comprehensive school in the centre of Wolverhampton, I cried all the way back to Yorkshire from the interview! Was it just because I would have to give up the green of the dales for the grey of industrial life, or was I subconsciously worried that, once back in Wolverhampton, I would lose my emerging new identity, and simply become my parents' child again? In these days of public disclosure, where spurned partners, in particular, seem quick to go to the media with embarrassing secrets about well-known personalities, it strikes me as a great blessing that parents are generally too loyal to their children to do the same, for if our mothers and fathers were to tell all, which one of us could stand?

However, although our parents and, to a lesser extent, the community in which we grew up, know more *about* our early years than anyone, it does not always follow that they know *us* better. Human beings – thank God – change and develop as they grow, but those with fixed ideas about the sort of person I am may be the last who are able to see the real me. Often, as in these verses, when people do not conform to what we know of them or expect of them we, like the folk of Nazareth, take offence. As they listened to Jesus preaching and teaching they were 'astounded', but something within them did not want to be taught by a local lad whom they had watched grow up, and their astonishment turned to rejection. Have we ever been guilty of similar reactions, when challenged by the faith or vision of our young people?

Mark goes on to tell us that, with a few exceptions, Jesus 'could do no deed of power there'. Because the residents of Nazareth could only see Jesus as they had always seen him, as 'the carpenter, the son of Mary', they were unable to see him through the eyes of faith, and to place their trust in him. Consequently, his power was limited by their unbelief. We are in a very different position from those Nazarenes who had watched Jesus grow up, and yet there is a danger that we can fall into a similar trap. Those of us who have grown up in Sunday School and in church may have allowed a certain picture of Jesus to become fixed in our minds, which can prevent us from seeing him in new ways as our lives change and our faith develops. Teaching Religious Education to secondary school students in the Caribbean I met resistance when I showed them African paintings depicting Jesus as black – 'That can't be Jesus, Miss, Jesus didn't look like that.' Further questioning revealed that they, like many of us, had been influenced by the kind of paintings hung in churches and by illustrations for children's religious books which were popular in previous generations. Despite their different cultural background, many still 'saw' Jesus as a blonde-haired white man, dressed in long floating white robes.

Of course, we are talking about much more than a visual image of Christ. What is vital is that our relationship with him changes and develops as we do. C. S. Lewis again expresses this very simply in *Prince Caspian* as Lucy meets up with Aslan the lion once again:

> 'Aslan,' said Lucy, 'you're bigger.'
> 'That is because you are older, little one,' answered he.
> 'Not because you are?'
> 'I am not. But every year you grow, you will find me bigger.'

Prayer:

Lord Jesus, I confess that I have sometimes rejected you and rejected your claims on my life because they did not fit in with the picture of you that I cherish, or with the childish images of you to which I cling. Help me to 'find you bigger' as I travel on this Lenten journey with you. Amen

Thursday   Mark 10:17-22
He went away grieving

As he was setting out on a journey, a man ran up and knelt before him, and asked him, 'Good Teacher, what must I do to inherit eternal life?' Jesus said to him, 'Why do you call me good? No one is good but God alone. You know the commandments: "You shall not murder; You shall not commit adultery; You shall not steal; You shall not bear false witness; You shall not defraud; Honour your father and mother." ' He said to him, 'Teacher, I have kept all these since my youth.' Jesus, looking at him, loved him and said, 'You lack one thing; go, sell what you own, and give the money to the poor, and you will have treasure in heaven; then come, follow me.' When he heard this, he was shocked and went away grieving, for he had many possessions.

➤ Perhaps, like me, you can remember all too well how it feels to be standing on a school playing-field, ankle-deep in mud and knees knocking from the cold as the chosen team captains pick their teams. Name after name is called, and it is absolutely no surprise to you to be left standing there until the bitter end, when, with a heavy sigh from the reluctant captain, you are finally selected and given the opportunity to show your dubious skills on the hockey field or football pitch!

➤ A few years later, you offer yourself again for rejection, as you apply to universities or colleges for a place to study, dreading the stark finality of rejection slips from all your choices.

➤ And by now, for many, members of the opposite sex have become infinitely fascinating and courage has to be found to issue an invitation to a school disco, or for a walk in the park – at least that's how it was in the 1970s – invitations which again carry a high risk of being met with rejection.

Life can be very painful for a teenager; and that doesn't stop as we leave adolescence behind. Job rejections, being passed over for promotion, marriage breakdown, conflicts with parents or children, disputes with neighbours or colleagues – all can leave us feeling battered, unwanted and rejected. One truth we can take from this story is that Jesus knows and understands about rejection. An earnest young man comes to Jesus with enthusiastic questions about developing his spiritual life; he clearly knows the law and tells Jesus that he has kept it since he 'knew himself' (as the Caribbean phrase puts it). Jesus, we are told, looked at him and loved him. How keenly he must have hoped that this able young man would take up the challenge he was about to throw at him and would join his band of disciples. But the price is too high; Jesus sees that the one thing holding this man back is his wealth and so that is what he puts his finger on, and he touches a nerve. Faced with the prospect of giving away his many possessions, the man cools off, turns his back on Jesus and walks away. Jesus felt the pain of that rejection.

As Lent progresses we often focus on other passages which tell of Jesus facing rejection; abandoned by his disciples; mocked and spat upon by soldiers; jeered at and slapped by religious leaders; handed over to death by politicians who knew better. Whatever rejections we may have faced in our lives, we can be sure that Jesus understands our pain, he has been there. What is more, he has come through to the glorious healing of resurrection and he can offer hope and consolation to us in our pain – rejection knocks us down but we do not have to stay down, for Christ stretches his hand out to us and wants to raise us up.

What became of the rich young man? Who knows? Perhaps he thought over the words of Jesus and came to the conclusion that Jesus was right after all; perhaps he did sell his belongings and find his life by losing it for the sake of Jesus . . . or perhaps he closed a door in his mind on what he had been told and tried to resume his life as before. Many of us do just that. When we feel Jesus is asking too much, the choice is always ours to turn and walk away.

Prayer:

Lord Jesus Christ, you have been with me in the many rejections of my life, large and small. You have stood by me and raised me up again. Now, during this Lenten season, I hear you asking for more of me, more of my love, more of my obedience, more of my will – give me grace to follow you, whatever the cost, and not to turn and walk away. Amen

Friday   **Mark 15:6-15**

Release Barabbas instead

Now at the festival he used to release a prisoner for them, anyone for whom they asked. Now a man called Barabbas was in prison with the rebels who had committed murder during the insurrection. So the crowd came and began to ask Pilate to do for them according to his custom. Then he answered them, 'Do you want me to release for you the King of the Jews?' For he realised that it was out of jealousy that the chief priests had handed him over. But the chief priests stirred up the crowd to have him release Barabbas for them instead. Pilate spoke to them again, 'Then what do you wish me to do with the man you call the King of the Jews?' They shouted back, 'Crucify him!' Pilate asked them, 'Why, what evil has he done?' But they shouted all the more, 'Crucify him!' So Pilate, wishing to satisfy the crowd, released Barabbas for them; and after flogging Jesus, he handed him over to be crucified.

Recent General Elections in Britain have not caused quite as much interest as our politicians might have hoped. Low turn-outs suggest a widespread indifference to all shades of political activism, and little hope that one party may govern any better than another. This is not the case in the Caribbean. Within a few weeks of our arrival in Chateaubelair in January 1994 a General Election was held. We could not believe the noise and excitement generated! Large political rallies were held almost nightly, and as the manse was on the central crossroads of the town, where everything took place, we had a bird's-eye view from our balcony. On Sunday afternoons, huge motorcades would travel the length of the island, truck after truck full of avid supporters, all wearing the standard issue party T-shirt, spending the whole day going from town to town for open-air rallies and speech-making. As Chateaubelair was almost at the end of the road along the Leeward coast of St. Vincent, scenes of chaos would ensue as the first vehicles, having turned round at Richmond beach, would come back into Chateaubelair before the later ones had passed. If the resultant traffic jams lasted for hours, who complained? It was all part of election fever!

Small-island politics is inevitably closely linked to personalities and there is bound to be much self-interest involved in the giving of political support. Charges of corruption and vote-buying were always levied following a result, by whichever side had lost, of course! Paul is wise to encourage us to pray for all who govern us, for politics in every part of the world must surely be a moral minefield.

Whenever there is a choice to be made or a vote to be cast, the danger is that those making the selection are motivated chiefly by self-interest. Political parties know this and appeal primarily to our pockets and our concerns about law and order or education rather than risk all with policies which promote, for example, a fairer or greener international community. Perhaps one of the few good things to have resulted from September 11th 2001 is a realisation that we must have a less parochial and more global perspective on many issues.

When Pilate offered the crowd the chance to release Jesus in the annual festival amnesty, the crowd had already been influenced by Jesus' enemies, the chief priests and religious leaders, to ask instead for Barabbas, a rebel and possible murderer. Perhaps bribes had been paid, perhaps inducements offered, or the threat of trouble for families who did not 'toe the party line' – the religious leaders of Jesus' day had a lot more power over people's lives than our ministers or even archbishops do today. Pilate himself, Mark tells us, could see that the chief priests' real motive in handing Jesus over was jealousy – another form of self-interest. Jesus' life and teaching seemed to the Jewish authorities to undermine their own importance and threaten their current status. Little did they realise that his death, which they so much desired, would establish an eternal priesthood that rendered theirs permanently redundant. Self-interest has a nasty way of paying us back!

Prayer:

I have been there, Lord, been there in the crowd which is only doing what it was told, thinking of myself before I think of what is right or just or better for all concerned. I have shouted 'Crucify' to your claims upon my life, and rejected you in favour of a less demanding option. Lord, have mercy. Amen

Saturday   **Isaiah 53:3-8**
Rejected by others

He was despised and rejected by others;
  a man of suffering and acquainted with infirmity;
    and as one from whom others hide their faces
      he was despised, and we held him of no account.
Surely he has borne our infirmities
  and carried our diseases;
    yet we accounted him stricken,
      struck down by God and afflicted.
But he was wounded for our transgressions,
  crushed for our iniquities;
    upon him was the punishment that made us whole,
      and by his bruises we are healed.
All we like sheep have gone astray;
  we have all turned to our own way,
    and the Lord has laid on him the iniquity of us all.
He was oppressed, and he was afflicted,
  yet he did not open his mouth;
    like a lamb that is led to the slaughter,
      and like a sheep that before its shearers is silent,
        so he did not open his mouth.
By a perversion of justice he was taken away.

➢ In March 1979, an almost bloodless coup overthrew the government of Grenada, which was taken over by a revolutionary party with massive national support, led by Maurice Bishop, an immensely popular leader.

➢ For four-and-a-half years Grenada developed under the new regime, modelled on Marxist principles. The infrastructure was improved, education and services upgraded although, by the end, a spirit of fear and suspicion prevailed.

➢ In October 1983 an internal split within the revolutionary party led to tragedy as Maurice Bishop, along with a number of his colleagues, were assassinated at Fort George. An unknown number of civilians died in the chaos that followed.

> On 25th October 1983 American and Caribbean forces landed in Grenada to restore democracy. This action is variously seen as 'invasion', 'intervention' or 'rescue'.

> Those seventeen members of the Central Committee – sixteen men and one woman – who were held responsible for the death of the Prime Minister and others were sentenced to hang, and were incarcerated in Richmond Hill Prison, St. George's, Grenada.

> After five years on 'death row' in solitary confinement, their sentences were transmuted to 'life, with hard labour'. With the exception of the one woman, who is now undergoing medical treatment on another island, they are still there. They have amazing stories to tell.

Leon tells of being taken outside to be executed, and of receiving news of the reduced sentence literally at the eleventh hour. He also speaks of beatings resulting in broken ribs, of the torture of spending years under a blazing light bulb – day and night.

Chris tells of standing, bound, to be tried in a kangaroo court and being spat upon – feeling the spittle running down his face and being powerless even to wipe it away.

A Methodist Local Preacher before the revolution, Leon turned away from a church that seemed ineffective in righting the wrongs in his land, to embrace socialism and then Marxism. After the bloodshed which ended the revolution he entered a period of deep questioning. He writes, 'As I tumbled into an abyss of meaninglessness, to my great surprise, God lovingly embraced me. I have experienced His forgiveness. I feel accepted and loved by Him.'

Bernard, a brilliant thinker and strategist, tells of his former conviction that people could be changed from the outside: 'Now,' he says, 'I have come to realise that people can only be changed from the inside.'

Living in the drab, grim, often brutal prison environment, this group of people are amongst the most alive, enthusiastic, Spirit-filled, caring men and women I have ever been privileged to meet.

Within the prison, these men do an amazing work of education, counselling and spiritual guidance. Some had wives and young children when they were first imprisoned, but are now divorced. Leon has taken a degree in Theology whilst in prison and feels a call to ministry . . .

Questions:

1. Think of recent news/media stories which have mentioned the church. How have they portrayed Christians and Christianity? How has that made you feel? Read Hebrews 12:2-3.

2. How do you feel about the suggestion that at times God may reject humanity? (see Tuesday). What alternatives are there for a God who gives free choice?

3. Have there been times in your life when you have rejected God? Are you rejecting God now? Is this serious? Are there some elements of your understating of God which you *should* reject, as individuals, or as a group or church?

Week 5: Serving

One of the primary pictures of humanity in relation to God throughout the Bible is that of a servant. Many of the heroes and heroines of the faith describe themselves as God's slaves. Perhaps this image is losing something of its appeal in the current climate, where we are constantly encouraged to take control of our own lives. To be in the 'serving professions' does not have the status or respect it once had, and our society is the poorer for that. Within the fields of both politics and the Church, we would do well to remember that 'minister' really means 'servant'!

Fifth Sunday in Lent   John 12:1-8
    Mary anointed Jesus' feet

Monday   Deuteronomy 15:12-17
    He shall be your slave forever

Tuesday   1 Kings 17:1-9
    I have commanded the ravens to feed you

Wednesday   2 Kings 5:19-27
    Your servant has not gone anywhere at all

Thursday   Luke 7:36-47
    You gave me no water for my feet, but she . . .

Friday   John 13:3-17
    You also should do as I have done to you

Saturday   Psalm 123:1-4
    The eyes of servants

Fifth Sunday in Lent   John 12:1-8
Mary anointed Jesus' feet

Six days before the Passover Jesus came to Bethany, the home of Lazarus, whom he had raised from the dead. There they gave a dinner for him. Martha served, and Lazarus was one of those at the table with him. Mary took a pound of costly perfume made of pure nard, anointed Jesus' feet, and wiped them with her hair. The house was filled with the fragrance of the perfume. But Judas Iscariot, one of the disciples (the one who was about to betray him), said, 'Why was this perfume not sold for three hundred denarii and the money given to the poor?' (He said this not because he cared about the poor, but because he was a thief; he kept the common purse and used to steal what was put into it.) Jesus said, 'Leave her alone. She bought it so that she might keep it for the day of my burial. You always have the poor with you, but you do not always have me.'

> Christ has many services to be done:
> some are easy, others are difficult;
> some bring honour, others bring reproach;
> some are suitable to our natural inclinations and material
>   interests,
> others are contrary to both;
> in some we may please Christ and please ourselves;
> in others we cannot please Christ except by denying
>   ourselves.
> Yet the power to do all these things is given to us in
>   Christ,
> who strengthens us.
>
> (*MWB* p288)

These words, from the Methodist Covenant Service, may bring to our minds the jobs that we really hope no one will ever ask us to do in church or in the community! These 'difficult' jobs will, of course, be different for different people; some great saints and 'backroom workers' may dread being asked to stand up and give a testimony or lead prayers, whilst others will relish those opportunities but hope no one suggests they join the cleaning rota . . . However, as we respond to this challenge by saying the words of the Covenant prayer we open ourselves to any and every kind of service for Christ. Throughout the Bible we find God calling the suitable and unsuitable alike; sometimes individuals seem ideal for their calling; they appear to have the right 'natural' gifts and make-up and God calls them to use their abilities in his service. Abraham could be seen as an example of this, as could David and, much later, Paul. Others, however, seem anything but suitable for the work to which they are called: Moses had a stammer, Gideon was timid, Samson had innumerable weaknesses and Elizabeth and Zechariah were well past normal parenting age! We neither can, nor should we try to, predict what God has in store for us.

In these verses from John, we meet three people with different ideas about serving Jesus:

➢ Martha looked after his physical needs and the needs of others as she served food.

➢ Mary, however, spent her time at the feet of Jesus, anointing him with very costly perfume and scenting the air of the whole house with the fragrance of the nard and of her devotion.

➢ Judas criticised Mary, suggesting that a more valid form of service would be to take action to help the poor (although John casts suspicion on his real motives).

How does Jesus react to these varying services offered to him?

➢ Luke, in a similar incident, records Jesus telling Martha that she has become too distracted by what needs to be done, she needs to grasp the importance of that service which can only be offered when the body is still and the mind is focused on God (Luke 10:41).

> To Judas, Jesus gives a challenge for, like Jesus himself, Judas would have been familiar with the books of the Law and with the words, 'Since then there will never cease to be some in need on the earth, I therefore command you, "Open your hand to the poor and needy neighbour in your land."' (Deuteronomy 15:11). If you say this is your concern, Judas, let's see you doing something about it personally!

> Mary, both here and in Luke 10, is wholeheartedly commended for her costly offering of love and devotion, for, unlike the food, so quickly consumed, and the alms-giving which can never be enough, what Mary is giving and receiving will not be taken away from her, but will last for ever. Especially in this Lenten season, let us not mistake action for anointing, or duties for devotion.

Prayer:

Lord Jesus, as I make my Covenant with you, saying that 'I am no longer my own, but yours', help me to lose all my preconceived ideas about serving you and to be open to your call, wherever that may lead me.
Amen

Monday   Deuteronomy 15: 12-17
He shall be your slave for ever

If a member of your community, whether a Hebrew man or a Hebrew woman, is sold to you and works for you for six years, in the seventh year you shall set that person free. And when you send a male slave out from you a free person, you shall not send him out empty-handed. Provide liberally out of your flock, your threshing-floor, and your wine press, thus giving to him some of the bounty with which the Lord your God has blessed you. Remember that you were a slave in the land of Egypt, and the Lord your God redeemed you; for this reason I lay this command upon you today. But if he says to you, 'I will not go out from you', because he loves you and your household, since he is well off with you, then you shall take an awl and thrust it through his earlobe into the door, and he shall be your slave for ever. You shall do the same with regard to your female slave.

Going as white 'missionaries' (even though we are now called 'mission partners') into a black community inevitably raised many questions for us. Throughout the two-year process of offering for overseas work, and particularly during the term we spent in training, Andrew and I were encouraged to think through the issues raised by a past of white domination and black slavery. Tragic events have taken place in history whenever one nation, race or colour has considered itself better than another, or assumed the right to order the lives and affairs of others. Those of us who are white can only be bitterly ashamed of what has been done.

When we arrived in Chateaubelair, we found a community very aware of its comparatively recent emergence from slavery. A close friend, seeing me recoil from eating the head (including eyes), bones and tail of the locally caught fish, told me without self-consciousness or rancour, 'We eat everything because those were the only parts given to our parents when they were slaves.' Black neighbours and friends told us themselves that their community suffered because of a 'slave mentality' which waited to be told what to do, and continually looked for guidance and aid from outside. The bitter legacy of slavery lives on today.

The existence of slavery within the Bible raises a huge and complex debate. However, from among the mass of references to slavery, some clear messages do emerge. One, mentioned in the verses above, is that the Israelites should never forget that they themselves were slaves in Egypt, and so the standards expected from Hebrew slave-masters are consistently higher than what was normal in surrounding cultures. This pattern is expanded in the New Testament, where Christian slave-owners are similarly called to demonstrate their new convictions in the way they treat their slaves.

These verses also introduce us to a little Old Testament foreshadowing of the Christian life. Some slaves, it is realised, because of their love for their owner and his household, and their appreciation of all that is theirs, will not wish to be set free. In these cases, the willing slave will have his ear pierced to show his status – he is a slave, but only because he chooses to be. Body piercing is no new invention, although it seems likely that its origin, as a mark of slavery, has been largely forgotten in the twenty-first century!

We who have accepted the yoke of Christ and offered ourselves in his service have done so of our own choice; God keeps no unwilling slaves in his household. Like the slave of Deuteronomy 15, we make this choice because we love God, because we want to belong to his family, the Church, and because we have been 'blessed in Christ with every spiritual blessing in the heavenly places' (Ephesians 1:3). God no longer thrusts his awl through our ear to mark this willing slavery, but, as Paul continues later in Ephesians 1, 'In him you also . . . were marked with the seal of the promised Holy Spirit' (v13).

Pierce my ear, O Lord my God.
Take me to Your throne this day.
I will serve no other god. Lord, I'm here to stay.

For You have paid the price for me.
With your blood You ransomed me.
I will serve you eternally, a free man I'll never be.

Steven Croft

Tuesday   1 Kings 17:1-9
I have commanded the ravens to feed you

Now Elijah the Tishbite, of Tishbe in Gilead said to Ahab, 'As the Lord the God of Israel lives, before whom I stand, there shall be neither dew nor rain these years, except by my word.' The word of the Lord came to him, saying, 'Go from here and turn eastwards, and hide yourself by the Wadi Cherith, which is east of the Jordan. You shall drink from the wadi, and I have commanded the ravens to feed you there.' So he went and did according to the word of the Lord; he went and lived by the Wadi Cherith, which is east of the Jordan. The ravens brought him bread and meat in the morning, and bread and meat in the evening; and he drank from the wadi. But after a while the wadi dried up, because there was no rain in the land. Then the word of the Lord came to him, saying, 'Go now to Zarephath, which belongs to Sidon, and live there; for I have commanded a widow there to feed you.'

Giving help is often easier than receiving it. Many of us like to be the strong ones, the capable ones who cope in any situation and are always there to give others a helping hand. Our motto is 'I can cope' and we aim never to show vulnerability or need in any way. I confess that I am rather like this myself, but, looking back, I realise that the periods in my life when I have been most at sea and in need of the help of others (such as after the birth of our first child; a few years later following a miscarriage, and in the early months overseas) are probably also the times when I have grown most.

Elijah was undoubtedly one of God's greatest servants. His life reads as a wonderful adventure, packed with miracles, political showdowns and daring feats of faith. He is used as God's instrument to predict a drought throughout Israel and beyond, while the faithless King Ahab is on the throne. He himself will be affected by this drought, for water and food are scarce everywhere. What is more, King Ahab is likely to be hunting for Elijah, the 'troubler of Israel' (as he calls him in 1 Kings 18:17). However, God has made provision for his servant; whilst there is still water to be found in one brook, Elijah is to hide there, and God has commanded ravens to bring him bread and meat morning and evening. Eventually even that source of water dries up, so God moves Elijah on, into the heathen territory of Sidon, to be fed, miraculously, by a poor widow in Zarephath.

As far as we can tell, Elijah gratefully accepted the arrangements made for him. He could have used John Wesley's own words, 'Let me be employed for you, or laid aside for you . . . let me have all things, let me have nothing' (*MWB* p290). Part of Elijah's greatness came through knowing when to let others help him. He is not above receiving food from birds or even from a foreign woman.

During our years in the South Caribbean, we were greatly helped by very many people. We needed help in understanding the people we lived amongst – not just in picking up and deciphering the strong local dialect of Chateaubelair, but, more importantly, in noticing and interpreting the more elusive signals of body language. We needed help in re-examining the gospel with which we were so familiar, in the light of a very different culture. We needed the regular prayers of our families and friends back in the UK, along with countless people we had never met who upheld us through the pages of the *Methodist Prayer Handbook*. I certainly needed help when presented with live chickens and not-long-dead fish to prepare and cook! Undoubtedly it was as we learned to ask for and accept help that we were strengthened, bridges were built and, perhaps, some of the age-old barriers between black and white began to be eroded.

Something about this story of Elijah always reminds me of another Bible verse, more commonly looked at in Lent. After Jesus' time in the wilderness Matthew writes, 'Then the devil left him, and suddenly angels came and waited on him' (Matthew 4:11). Jesus himself, the Son of God, the King of kings and the Lord of lords, both needed and accepted help. As we look for opportunities to serve God and others in our lives, let us also be open to receiving service, for that is part of God's plan for how we should live.

> **Brother, Sister, let me serve you,**
> **let me be as Christ to you;**
> **Pray that I may have the grace**
> **to let you be my servant too.**
>
> Richard Gillard

Wednesday   2 Kings 5:19-27
Your servant has not gone anywhere at all

The Syrian army commander, Naaman, has been healed from leprosy by Elisha, and sets off home:

But when Naaman had gone from him a short distance, Gehazi, the servant of Elisha the man of God, thought, 'My master has let that Aramean Naaman off too lightly by not accepting from him what he offered. As the Lord lives, I will run after him and get something out of him.' So Gehazi went after Naaman. When Naaman saw someone running after him, he jumped down from the chariot to meet him and said, 'Is everything all right?' He replied, 'Yes, but my master has sent me to say, "Two members of a company of prophets have just come to me from the hill country of Ephraim; please give them a talent of silver and two changes of clothing." ' Naaman said, 'Please accept two talents.' He urged him, and tied up two talents of silver in two bags, with two changes of clothing, and gave them to two of his servants, who carried them in front of Gehazi. When he came to the citadel, he took the bags from them, and stored them inside; he dismissed the men and they left.

He went in and stood before his master; and Elisha said to him, 'Where have you been, Gehazi?' He answered, 'Your servant has not gone anywhere at all.' But he said to him, 'Did I not go with you in spirit when someone left his chariot to meet you? Is this a time to accept money and to accept clothing, olive orchards and vineyards, sheep and oxen, and male and female slaves? Therefore the leprosy of Naaman shall cling to you, and to your descendants for ever.' So he left his presence leprous, as white as snow.

Gehazi was neither the first nor the last servant to think he knew better than his master. Galled by Elisha's refusal to accept a fee of any sort from the healed Naaman, Gehazi determines to obtain a little private income from the largesse of this important foreigner. He catches up with Naaman and invents a story about unexpected guests, claiming that Elisha himself has sent him with this request. Naaman obliges and, in addition, sends his own servants to carry the goods back for Gehazi – suddenly the servant has become the master, and we can imagine how much he enjoyed his new role, as the two men walk in front of him with their burdens, until he dismisses them and hides away his booty!

It seems that this sudden greed has caused Gehazi to forget that his master is a prophet – a seer indeed, whose very calling it was to see what others could not see and to know what was otherwise known only to God. From inside his home, Elisha has 'seen' all that has taken place and a lot more besides! He questions Gehazi about his movements and Gehazi replies, 'Your servant has not gone anywhere at all.' Of course, this is a familiar Hebrew pattern of speech, meaning, 'I have not gone anywhere at all'; but in an ironic way his words hold a deeper truth – as Elisha's servant, Gehazi has not gone anywhere. The journey he made to catch up with Naaman was made entirely as his own master.

Gehazi fell into the simple trap of forgetting he was only a servant. He over-stepped the boundaries of his position and went directly against his master's will. Doubtless he would have seen what he did as harmless enough; the goods had been freely offered, his actions could not be understood as theft, simply as sensible provision against 'a rainy day'. Elisha sees further, however. Elisha sees much that has not yet happened but which may happen if Gehazi's greed is unchecked. As Elisha chastises his servant he mentions not only the money and clothing which Gehazi has already received, but also goes on to enumerate some other desires of his servant's heart – land, cattle, slaves of his own – which might have become the next stages of his dishonesty.

If we look at this story as an illustration of our own servant relationship to God, we may be able to identify times in our lives when we have sought after something which we really knew was not God's will for us. We may have believed that it will do us no harm, we may have consciously made the decision to forget, for a time, who is master, and to do as we please. Gehazi suffered the consequences of his actions, and so did his family after him. This may seem harsh and hard to reconcile with a God of forgiveness, but who knows from what depravity Gehazi was saved as his master reasserted his rightful control over him?

> **Make me a captive, Lord,**
>   **And then I shall be free;**
> **Force me to render up my sword,**
>   **And I shall conqueror be.**
> **I sink in life's alarms**
>   **When by myself I stand;**
> **Imprison me within thine arms,**
>   **And strong shall be my hand.**

George Matheson
HP 714

Thursday   Luke 7:36-47
You gave me no water for my feet, but she . . .

One of the Pharisees asked Jesus to eat with him, and he went into the Pharisee's house and took his place at the table. And a woman in the city, who was a sinner, having learned that he was eating in the Pharisee's house, brought an alabaster jar of ointment. She stood behind him at his feet, weeping, and began to bathe his feet with her tears and to dry them with her hair. Then she continued kissing his feet and anointing them with the ointment. Now when the Pharisee who had invited him saw it, he said to himself, 'If this man were a prophet, he would have known who and what kind of woman this is who is touching him – that she is a sinner.' Jesus spoke up and said to him, 'Simon, I have something to say to you.' 'Teacher,' he replied, 'speak.' 'A certain creditor had two debtors; one owed five hundred denarii, and the other fifty. When they could not pay, he cancelled the debts for both of them. Now which of them will love him more?' Simon answered, 'I suppose the one for whom he cancelled the greater debt.' And Jesus said to him, 'You have judged rightly.' Then turning towards the woman he said to Simon, 'Do you see this woman? I entered your house; you gave me no water for my feet, but she has bathed my feet with her tears and dried them with her hair. You gave me no kiss, but from the time I came in she has not stopped kissing my feet. You did not anoint my head with oil, but she has anointed my feet with ointment. Therefore, I tell you, her sins, which were many, have been forgiven; hence she has shown great love. But the one to whom little is forgiven, loves little.'

This story, similar in some respects to Sunday's passage, is, to me, all about perception. Simon is disappointed in Jesus' lack of perception regarding the lifestyle of the unnamed woman. However, it is the striking contrast between the perceptions of Simon and of the woman, concerning Jesus, that makes the story.

Perhaps one of the worst feelings of all is the feeling that you have outstayed your welcome somewhere, or that you were never welcome in the first place. Jesus' words to Simon make it clear that there had been a glaring omission of every normal form of welcome on this occasion. Simon invited Jesus to his home, but shows by his actions that he has not perceived the significance of Jesus' presence, and the service he offers to his guest is no service at all.

The woman, on the other hand, has perceived that Jesus is someone special. She has deliberately sought him out in order to offer him the very best service she can. Risking reproach, she responds extravagantly to his presence, with tears and ointment.

Perceiving, or failing to perceive, the significance of God's presence is still a matter of ultimate importance. The world is full of people who see the beauty of creation, but do not know who to thank for it; who appreciate love and laughter within human life, but have not understood that it is God who is the origin of all love and delight. As Christians, we should be like people in a supermarket who have suddenly noticed a famous celebrity trying to do their shopping incognito and who excitedly point them out to all around. We are those who have had our eyes opened to God's presence within his world and who cannot resist pointing this out to others. Taking a few moments out of busy lives to notice a sunset, wonder at a flower, express gratitude for a kindness or appreciation for someone's care can lift our spirits, help to open our neighbours' eyes, and bring glory to God.

God is not confined to church buildings nor even to Christian communities. God is on the terraces of our football stadiums, in the aisles of our supermarkets, in the struggling banana plantations and among the beach vendors of the Caribbean.

When we perceive the presence of Christ in every part of our lives, and celebrate that presence with the love and joy of the woman in this story, then we are offering him a vital service.

Prayer:

Lord God, I praise you because your presence surrounds me and fills your world. I confess that too often I have been like Simon, and not celebrated that presence, not offered you worthy service. Open my eyes today to see you, open my heart to love you and open my mouth to share you. In Jesus' name. Amen

Friday   John 13:3-17

You also should do as I have done to you

During supper Jesus, knowing that the Father had given all things into his hands, and that he had come from God and was going to God, got up from the table, took off his outer robe and tied a towel around himself. Then he poured water into a basin and began to wash the disciples' feet and to wipe them with the towel that was tied around him . . . After he had washed their feet, had put on his robe, and had returned to the table, he said to them, 'Do you know what I have done to you? You call me Teacher and Lord – and you are right, for that is what I am. So if I, your Lord and Teacher, have washed your feet, you also ought to wash one another's feet. For I have set you an example, that you also should do as I have done to you. Very truly, I tell you, servants are not greater than their master, nor are messengers greater than the one who sent them. If you know these things, you are blessed if you do them.'

We can all imagine the scene; as the disciples gather for this special supper together, it becomes apparent that no slave has been engaged to wash their feet before they eat. Perhaps they glanced around at each other, calculating who was the lowest in rank among them, who should perform this humble, rather unsavoury, duty? Perhaps each one felt that it was certainly not *his* job to do it, so no one did it; they reclined and began their meal. Some of us may have had similar feelings after a church meeting or social when, suddenly, the room is empty of people and there are all the chairs to put away, and the floor to sweep . . . 'Why should I?'

By his actions Jesus puts the disciples (and us) to shame; quietly he takes up the towel and basin and moves around the room, washing the feet of each disciple in turn. I imagine the room went very quiet, no one knowing quite what to say, only Peter daring to protest (see vv6-11, not printed above). Years ago, I worked for a while in a department store in Luton. Each Christmas it was the tradition in that store for the sales assistants, cleaners and stock-room staff to sit down in the shop restaurant for a full Christmas dinner (after hours) and to be served by the management. It was an interesting experience; a few of the 'underlings' took full advantage of the situation, ordering their superiors around with great gusto, but most of us felt slightly uncomfortable.

Jesus performed a humble service at the supper, and made a powerful point; one which the disciples would surely never forget. No one is too great to serve others. No work is too mundane, too humble, too unnoticed for the servant of Christ. Indeed, any service, however unpleasant and messy it might be, may be our opportunity to anoint the feet of Jesus with perfume, and the sweet smell of that service will spread far and wide. The way of Jesus calls us to break away from society's understanding of 'status' and live radically. When we first went to the West Indies, we were surprised to find ourselves in a culture which held Methodist ministers in high esteem! Ministers were not expected to help fix the church property, ministers' wives were not expected to clean their own homes. There were certainly temptations to go along with this, but Jesus' words are salutary; 'servants are not greater than their master' – if Jesus took it upon himself to serve others, we who are his servants must do the same.

There is a word here, too, for those who are in positions of authority over others – Jesus is the master who never exploits; his life gives us not only a model of servanthood, but also a model of 'mastery'. Relationships between servants and those they serve do not need to be exploitative; I have dined in large West Indian houses, where servants prepared and served the food, but those whom they served would later be in the kitchen alongside their servants, listening to them, caring for them, providing for them, serving them, in fact.

A deeper question, which it is appropriate to ask ourselves in this Lenten season, is: 'In my relationship with God, am I serving him, or is he serving me?'

Sometimes, especially in my prayers, I begin to find myself treating God as little more than a genie in a lamp, someone who will come at my beck and call and fix the muddles I find myself in. This is a far cry from being a 'slave of Christ', as Paul so often described himself.

> **Kneels at the feet of his friends,**
> **Silently washes their feet,**
> **Master who acts as a slave to them.**
> > *Jesu, Jesu*
> > *Fill us with your love,*
> > *Show us how to serve*
> > *The neighbours we have from you.*

T. S. Colvin
HP 145

Saturday   **Psalm 123:1-4**

The eyes of servants

To you I lift up my eyes,
   O you who are enthroned in the heavens!
As the eyes of servants look to the hand of their master,
      as the eyes of a maid to the hand of her mistress,
         so our eyes look to the Lord our God,
            until he has mercy upon us.
Have mercy upon us, O Lord, have mercy upon us,
      for we have had more than enough of contempt.
Our soul has had more than its fill
      of the scorn of those who are at ease,
         of the contempt of the proud.

➢ We all know how frustrating it is to be on the receiving end of inattentive service; the waiter whose eye we can never catch; the shop assistant who is so busy talking to a colleague that our requests go unheard; the office junior who doesn't listen and so pins confidential reports to the notice-board while shredding the weekly bulletin . . .

➢ A good servant, on the other hand, is always attentive, watching for the slightest signal from the 'boss' that something is required. This servant will not be found sleeping on the job, or be so engaged in his/her own activities – whether in thoughts, words or deeds – not to notice a summons.

➢ These verses have their root in a practice – still alive in some cultures today – where servants, or, in some cases, wives, keep their eyes fixed on the hand of the master or husband, watching for the gentle slap on the table which indicates that something is required.

As the eyes of servants look to the hand of their master,
as the eyes of a maid look to the hand of her mistress,
so our eyes look to the Lord our God.

The psalmist describes our relationship with God in just this way; our eyes constantly open and watching for any sign, any invitation to serve, any command to 'Come' or to 'Go'.

How attentive am I to the Lord my God?

How responsive am I when I sense God's invitation?

Our soul has had more than its fill of the scorn of those who are at ease, of the contempt of the proud.

Occasionally the world at large may be challenged by a life of humble service and devotion, as seen in Mother Teresa of Calcutta, for example. Generally, however, we should not expect this attitude of service to lead to acclaim from others; indeed, it is more likely to lead to scorn and contempt. Service is not seen as a route to greatness by our post-Christian cultures.

How willing am I to sacrifice greatness in the eyes of the world, to be a slave of Christ?

How do I feel when others pour scorn on the way I live my life . . .

the way I spend my money . . .

the way I bring up my children . . .

the way I speak to my students, my staff or my colleagues?

But it is not so among you; but whoever wishes to become great among you must be your servant, and whoever wishes to be first among you must be slave of all. For the Son of Man came not to be served but to serve, and to give his life a ransom for many.

Mark 10:43-45

Questions:

1. In these days of a culture of self-determination and self-awareness, is it still relevant to talk of Christians as 'slaves of Christ'? To what extent do you consider yourself to be a slave or a servant of God?

2. How do you feel about others serving you? Can you accept it graciously, or do you rebel?

3. Have you ever said 'Why should I?' (see Friday) Have you found that 'perfect liberty' (*HP* 534) which can come through service, or does the yoke still rub and give you blisters? What is the way forward?

Holy Week: Motives

As we enter Holy Week, we sense the impending climax of the story. This is a very special week, although I have noticed since our return to the UK, that it no longer receives much media attention. Until relatively recently, at least the *Radio Times* could be relied upon to have a religious cover for Holy Week, but no longer it seems! Opening its pages, too, I notice fewer and fewer programmes which mark this important time in the Christian calendar.

Whilst the posters with which we used to be issued at church on Palm Sunday when I was a child, showing a crucified Christ and proclaiming, 'This is Holy Week', were (even then) somewhat old-fashioned, nevertheless they provided a reminder to a busy world of the love and sacrifice of God.

So this week we step up the pace a bit, and the readings are longer. Throughout the week we will be looking at some key figures involved in the arrest, trial and sentencing of Jesus. Alongside these well-known passages we shall read Old Testament stories where people acted in a similar way. As we examine their possible motives for acting as they did, we shall observe that human nature still displays the same weaknesses in the twenty-first century, and so ask questions about our own motives as Christ's disciples.

Throughout this week you may want to ask yourself or discuss with others how you mark Holy Week in your devotional life, family life, church life. Perhaps it is not too early to make some plans for next year!

Palm Sunday   John 12:12-19 & 1 Samuel 18:5-9
    Jealousy

Monday   Matthew 26:14-16 & Genesis 37:23-28
    Personal Gain

Tuesday   Matthew 27:19-26 & Esther 3:8-11
   Weakness

Wednesday   Luke 23:6-12 & Numbers 22:1-6
   Control

Maundy Thursday   Luke 22:54-62 & Genesis 32: 6-8; 24-31
   Fear

Good Friday   John 19:16-20 & Genesis 22:1-8
   Obedience

Holy Saturday
   Love   Luke 23:52-56 & Song of Solomon 2:10-13 & 3:1-3

Palm Sunday

John 12:12-19 & 1 Samuel 18:5-9
Jealousy

The next day the great crowd that had come to the festival heard that Jesus was coming to Jerusalem. So they took branches of palm trees and went out to meet him, shouting, 'Hosanna! Blessed is the one who comes in the name of the Lord – the King of Israel!' Jesus found a young donkey and sat on it; as it is written: 'Do not be afraid, daughter of Zion. Look, your king is coming, sitting on a donkey's colt!'

His disciples did not understand these things at first; but when Jesus was glorified, then they remembered that these things had been written of him and had been done to him. So the crowd that had been with him when he called Lazarus out of the tomb and raised him from the dead continued to testify. It was also because they heard that he had performed this sign that the crowd went to meet him. The Pharisees then said to one another, 'You see, you can do nothing! Look, the world has gone after him!'

Today is a high point in the Christian calendar, a day, very often, of public processions and open-air gatherings. It is a day for standing up and shouting out – for pledging our allegiance to Christ and acknowledging him as King. In our worship today, we join with the countless thousands who will be shouting, 'Hosanna to the Son of David! Blessed is he who comes in the name of the Lord – the King of Israel.' Some will be waving real branches of palm trees, cut from the road side; others may have to make do with green crêpe paper taped to garden sticks; some will be riding real donkeys, as they do every day, others may have to imagine that part. But as our shouts join together, may our worldwide unity bring praise and glory to our King.

However, as we look behind the scenes on that first Palm Sunday, we see that not everyone was celebrating. Looking back a thousand years before Jesus' entry into Jerusalem, we can find a story with many parallels . . .

David went out and was successful wherever Saul sent him; as a result, Saul set him over the army. And all the people, even the servants of Saul, approved. As they were coming home, when David returned from killing the Philistine, the women came out of all the towns of Israel, singing and dancing, to meet King Saul, with tambourines, with songs of joy, and with musical instruments. And the women sang to one another as they made merry, 'Saul has killed his thousands, and David his tens of thousands.'

Saul was very angry, for this saying displeased him. He said, 'They have ascribed to David tens of thousands, and to me they have ascribed thousands; what more can he have but the kingdom?' So Saul eyed David from that day on.

Success breeds popularity:

➢ Jesus, having raised Lazarus from the dead, and having done many other wonderful things throughout Israel, became a popular hero. Hearing that he was to enter Jerusalem, the capital city, shortly before the busy feast of Passover, when all devout Jews would be gathering there, those who had seen him raise Lazarus, along with those who had heard about it, formed a great crowd and went out to meet him, to sing and shout and wave palm branches. Jesus, riding on a young donkey, seemed in every way to be the coming Messiah the people longed for – the King who, like David, would make Israel great again.

➢ David, who had killed Goliath and had had many other military victories, also became the national hero. King Saul was still acclaimed, of course; he was the king, and the crowds went out to meet him as befitted his arrival.

However, in the words of their songs, Saul's triumphs were eclipsed tenfold by those of David – David was number one now.

Popularity, however, breeds jealousy:

> The Jewish hierarchy, in contrast, had never been among Jesus' greatest fans. All four gospel writers give indications throughout their gospels that, from the standpoint of the official Jewish religion of the day, Jesus was 'public enemy number one'. However, if Jesus had stayed in the obscurity of Nazareth, it is unlikely that the religious leaders would have bothered much about him; if his message had been ignored by all but a few, they would not have felt threatened. But here is Jesus boldly entering Jerusalem itself, and receiving great public acclaim – the Pharisees confer hopelessly; it seems that the whole world is now following Jesus. Their position is threatened; they feel insecure and jealous.

> Saul had been only too pleased to find a young man who would fight Goliath for him, and, at first, he too delighted in David – a man whose good looks, courage, integrity and devotion to God had won the hearts of his own family, and of the people. However, as David takes first place in the nation's heart, he, unwittingly, provokes the jealousy of an insecure king. Saul is resentful of the sentiments of street ditties being sung in praise of David, and, we read, he begins to 'eye' him from that day.

Jealousy is an ugly emotion, perhaps not something we want to consider on this festival day. However, if we want to be amongst the crowd proclaiming Jesus as King today, we have to remember that, as Charles Wesley writes in the hymn, 'All glory to God in the sky', in the Kingdom of Christ, anger, hatred, envy, malice and discord are banished.

Come then to thy servants again,
Who long thy appearing to know;
Thy quiet and peaceable reign
In mercy establish below;
All sorrow before thee shall fly,
And anger and hatred be o'er,
And envy and malice shall die,
And discord afflict us no more.

Charles Wesley
HP 400

Although there should be no room for jealousy within our lives and within the Christian community, is this always so?

➤ Have we ever felt jealous when we hear of another church in our area, perhaps of a different denomination, attracting large congregations and even numbering young people among its members?

➤ Have we ever felt jealous when someone else is appointed to a role within church life which we have filled for years; especially if that person is actually making a better job of it than we did?

➤ Have we ever felt jealous of Christians in another country? Christians from rich nations might imagine it would be easier to be a Christian in a land without so much wealth and consumerism. Christians in developing lands might look at 'developed' lands and imagine it must be easier to be a Christian in a land where there are so many Christian resources – books, teaching aids, training, conventions.

➤ Have we ever felt jealous of the love and devotion our spouse, or our children, or our parents give to Christ himself, feeling insecure because we fear that we are not number one?

Prayer:

On this triumphant Sunday, Lord Jesus, King of Israel and my King, I come to you as I am – one individual amongst a throng of worshippers – and offer my shouts of joy and devotion. As Holy Week begins and you set before me the example of the Creator God riding on a lowly donkey, give me grace to conquer the jealousy and sin in my life with the humility of love and the meekness of obedience. Amen

Monday   Matthew 26:14-16 & Genesis 37:23-28
Personal Gain

Then one of the twelve, who was called Judas Iscariot, went to the chief priests and said, 'What will you give me if I betray him to you?' They paid him thirty pieces of silver. And from that moment he began to look for an opportunity to betray him.

So when Joseph came to his brothers, they stripped him of his robe, the long robe with sleeves that he wore; and they took him and threw him into a pit. The pit was empty; there was no water in it. Then they sat down to eat; and looking up they saw a caravan of Ishmaelites coming from Gilead, with their camels carrying gum, balm and resin, on their way to carry it down to Egypt. Then Judah said to his brothers, 'What profit is it if we kill our brother and conceal his blood? Come, let us sell him to the Ishmaelites, and not lay our hands on him, for he is our brother, our own flesh.' And his brothers agreed. When some Midianite traders passed by, they drew Joseph up, lifting him out of the pit, and sold him to the Ishmaelites for twenty pieces of silver. And they took Joseph to Egypt.

'Marrying for money' has been a feature of most cultures, in most centuries; whether it is the impoverished young girl who dazzles a wealthy older man, or the well-bred but impecunious hero of a Jane Austen novel who makes sure he knows the size of the dowry on offer before he selects his bride to be!

Openly or discreetly, many people, on entering a new relationship, whether personal or professional, ask themselves, 'What may be in this for me? How am I going to profit from this?' If we are honest, even our approach to Christ has something of this element in it. Although Jesus' own words about following him speak of taking up a cross and denying oneself, there have been those throughout the centuries who have preferred to preach a gospel of 'Come to Jesus and all your problems will disappear.' Of course, there *are* enormous blessings in store as we accept Christ into our lives and walk his way through life, so it is not always easy to disentangle the many strands which have bound us to him.

Joseph seems to have been a particularly obnoxious younger brother. He exploited his position as his father's favourite, 'telling tales' of his brothers and boasting of his remarkable dreams in which, it appeared, they all bowed down to him. Small wonder that the brothers decide to do away with him, initially planning to murder him, but then changing their plans as Judah asks, 'What profit is it if we kill our brother?' Maybe his own chief motive was to save Joseph's life, but he used the motivation of personal gain to persuade his brothers to go along with this, and their father's much-beloved son is exchanged for a mere twenty pieces of silver.

Judas had been one of Jesus' small band of disciples, and his name is mentioned in Mark's list of 'those whom Jesus wanted' (Mark 3:13-19). According to John he was the keeper of the common purse (John 13:29), a position of trust and responsibility; although John also describes him as a thief, suggesting that his criticism of Mary's generous anointing of Jesus was not really motivated by concern for the poor, but by personal greed (John 12:6). Perhaps there is enough evidence for us to conclude that Judas did have a weakness where money was concerned, a weakness which was then exploited as he saw the hostility of the chief priests towards Jesus, and the opportunity to make money from the situation. No doubt there were other motives at work too, deeper motives of jealousy, disappointment, frustration, disillusionment . . .

For us, perhaps the issue is even more complex and entangled, but there are ways in which we, like Judas, can be tempted to 'sell' Jesus:

➤ In business, opportunities may arise to boost the profits in particular ways, but these may involve a moral compromise; the exploitation of some other person or group; the inaccurate completion of financial records; even a bribe or 'back-hander'. Do we agree to betray the holy demands of Jesus for profit?

➤ In our domestic finances, as we complete our tax returns and other documents, even our gift-aid forms, are we scrupulously honest, or do we give in to the temptation to gain a little more money, even though this means compromising Jesus' standard of honesty?

➤ If we are undercharged in a shop or restaurant, do we point out the error and pay the full amount, or consider it must be our 'lucky day', and say nothing, silently betraying our Lord for a few silver coins?

➤ When Judas pretended a concern for the poor, whilst hoping that he would thereby benefit (John 12), was this so very different from the reference I recently heard on the radio to the 'generosity' of those who buy lottery tickets?

➤ A modern version of *The Pilgrim's Progress* introduces us to the character 'Owen Ends', a man who encourages Christian in his journey, telling him how his own business has prospered because others know him to be honest. He boasts that women love him too, feeling they can trust him. In the end, however, Owen Ends goes too close to the mine of Filthy Lucre and falls to his death. Self-interest is not the motivation for discipleship.

➤ It is not only about money, of course. Personal gain can be offered in many tempting guises – in each case perhaps we should examine our motives before we act.

Who was the guilty?   Who brought this upon
thee?
Alas, my treason, Jesus, hath undone thee.
'Twas I, Lord Jesus, I it was denied thee:
I crucified thee.

Robert Bridges
HP 164

When I survey the wondrous cross,
    On which the Prince of Glory died,
My richest gain I count but loss,
    And pour contempt on all my pride.

Were the whole realm of nature mine,
    That were a present far too small;
Love so amazing, so divine,
    Demands my soul, my life, my all.

Isaac Watts
HP 180

Prayer:

Lord Jesus, you allowed sinful men to betray you and to kill you, seeking only to do your Father's will and to lay down your life in obedience. Come to me, I pray, when my mind and heart are tempted to compromise you in order to gain something for myself. Release me from the lure of money, status and popularity, that I may be free to follow and love you for yourself alone. Amen

Tuesday   Matthew 27:19-26 & Esther 3:8-11
Weakness

While [Pilate] was sitting on the judgement seat, his wife sent word to him, 'Have nothing to do with that innocent man, for today I have suffered a great deal because of a dream about him.' Now the chief priests and the elders persuaded the crowds to ask for Barabbas and to have Jesus killed. . . . So when Pilate saw that he could do nothing, but rather that a riot was beginning, he took some water and washed his hands before the crowd, saying, 'I am innocent of this man's blood; see to it yourselves.' Then the people as a whole answered, 'His blood be on us and on our children!' So he released Barabbas for them; and after flogging Jesus, he handed him over to be crucified.

In this story from the Persian court of the fifth century BC, the king's favourite, Haman, launches an attack on the Jews throughout the Persian Empire:

Then Haman said to King Ahasuerus, 'There is a certain people scattered and separated among the peoples in all the provinces of your kingdom; their laws are different from those of every other people, and they do not keep the king's laws, so that it is not appropriate for the king to tolerate them. If it pleases the king, let a decree be issued for their destruction, and I will pay ten thousand talents of silver into the hands of those who have charge of the king's business, so that they may put it into the king's treasuries.' So the king took his signet ring from his hand and gave it to Haman, son of Hammedatha the Agagite, the enemy of the Jews. The king said to Haman, 'The money is given to you, and the people as well, to do with them as it seems good to you.'

Reading more of the book of Esther, we discover that the reason Haman wanted to destroy the Jews was that one particular Jew, Esther's uncle, Mordecai, persistently refused to bow to Haman whenever he passed. Piqued by this, Haman abused his position of intimacy with the king, to order a mass destruction of all Jews across the Persian Empire. Reading still further, we are glad to discover that his plans fail, indeed, they completely backfire and Haman himself ends up swinging from the gibbet he had had erected for Mordecai, while Mordecai is honoured as a national hero. In all of this, however, what is the role of King Ahasuerus? He, not Haman, is supposed to be in charge – does he really know what is going on? It seems not, until Queen Esther reveals the plot, claiming her own kinship with the threatened Jewish people.

Pilate, too, shows weakness; almost certainly he believed Jesus to be innocent, and this was further reinforced by the message from his wife. Is it even possible that Pilate, although a Gentile, knew of the Jewish law which provided for the purging of the guilt of innocent blood, and hoped that somehow he might absolve himself by imitating it? In the law (Deuteronomy 21:1-9) a heifer's neck is broken in a stream, and the elders 'wash their hands over the heifer whose neck was broken in the wadi, and they shall declare, "Our hands did not shed this blood, nor were we witnesses to it."' However, generations of Christendom have not absolved Pilate; his name remains the one historical reference in all major creeds as we confess that Jesus 'suffered under Pontius Pilate'.

Weakness in high places has led to innumerable tragedies and injustices on a world scale. Most of us, however, are not kings or governors; our daily work does not generally present us with choices that could mean life or death to someone else; nor do we have high-ranking officials pressing us to set our seal upon vital documents. Weakness can hardly be seen as a motive for anything. By its very nature it is not strong enough to motivate us, but it can sap our determination to do what is right, to be the sort of people who make a difference in our homes, workplaces and communities. Are we, like Ahasuerus and Pilate, ever guilty of allowing weakness to lead us into actions which harm others and denigrate Christ?

➢ Do we sometimes shirk from accepting responsibility, at work or at home? Would we prefer someone else to take the messy decisions about union action, or staff redundancies or disciplining the children, so that we can feel absolved of any blame?

➢ Have we ever signed papers that we haven't read in detail, because we didn't have time, or we couldn't be bothered, or we didn't really care?

➢ In church, have we allowed situations to develop or continue which are unhealthy – minor feuds, disagreements, misunderstandings which cause pain and which damage the unity and mission of the Church. Is it weakness which has prevented us from speaking out, from making amends, from trying to bring about reconciliation?

➢ Taking it further, have we considered how our shopping patterns can affect the lives of others – do we make the effort to buy fairly-traded goods where possible, to ask for Caribbean bananas[1]; to boycott unethical companies and support local producers, or is all this too much effort?

Lent, and in particular Holy Week, is a good time for a spiritual check-up. We may well discover we have more weaknesses than we realised! This is the time to bring ourselves honestly before the God who, in Christ, experienced the weakness of human flesh and who waits to fill us with his strength day by day.

> **When my love to Christ grows weak,**
> **When for deeper faith I seek,**
> **Then in thought I go to thee,**
> **Garden of Gethsemane.**

When my love for man grows weak,
When for stronger faith I seek,
Hill of Calvary, I go
To thy scenes of fear and woe.

Then to life I turn again,
Learning all the worth of pain,
Learning all the might that lies
In a full self-sacrifice.

John Reynell Wreford
HP 183

Prayer:

Lord Jesus, in your incarnate life upon this planet, you took on frail, human flesh in all its weakness and yet you lived a life without sin. Too often I allow my weaknesses to lead me into sin, to mar my witness for you, to hamper my role in your mission. Help me to recognise my own areas of weakness, so that I may come to you to be filled with your strength. Thank you that, however often I fall, you do not wash your hands of me, but raise me up in new life and hope. Amen

1   The 'banana war' launched at the World Trade Organisation in 1998 by the US required the EU to end the concessions it gave to small-scale Caribbean banana farmers, forcing them to compete on the open market with large US companies. Such a step, with which Christian Aid say the EU will have to comply in time, is seriously threatening the livelihoods of many Caribbean banana growers. Britain was amongst the countries which encouraged many islands of the Caribbean to grow bananas – do we not have a responsibility to support this fragile market?

Wednesday

Luke 23:6-12 & Numbers 22:1-6
Control

Pilate . . . asked whether the man was a Galilean. And when he learned that he was under Herod's jurisdiction, he sent him off to Herod, who was himself in Jerusalem at that time. When Herod saw Jesus, he was very glad, for he had been wanting to see him for a long time, because he had heard about him and was hoping to see him perform some sign. He questioned him at some length, but Jesus gave him no answer. The chief priests and the scribes stood by, vehemently accusing him. Even Herod with his soldiers treated him with contempt and mocked him; then he put an elegant robe on him, and sent him back to Pilate. That same day Herod and Pilate became friends with each other; before this they had been enemies.

The Israelites set out, and camped in the plains of Moab across the Jordan from Jericho. Now Balak, son of Zippor saw all that Israel had done to the Amorites. Moab was in great dread of the people, because they were so numerous; Moab was overcome with fear of the people of Israel. And Moab said to the elders of Midian, 'This horde will now lick up all that is around us, as an ox licks up the grass of the field.' Now Balak son of Zippor was king of Moab at that time. He sent messengers to Balaam son of Beor at Pethor, which is on the Euphrates, in the land of Amaw, to summon him, saying, 'A people has come out of Egypt; they have spread over the face of the earth, and they have settled next to me. Come now, curse this people for me, since they are stronger than I; perhaps I shall be able to defeat them and drive them from the land; for I know that whomsoever you bless is blessed, and whomsoever you curse is cursed.'

The story of **Balak and Balaam** is fascinating. Frightened by the might of Israel, King Balak of Moab tries to force the prophet Balaam to curse the Israelites. Balaam himself is not a Hebrew, so his very status as a prophet who, as the story goes on, receives direct revelations from the Lord God of Israel, is surprising. However, Balaam does not fall in with Balak's plans, for the Lord gives him only words of blessing for Israel. What we are looking at here is Balak's desire to 'use' God, to employ the forces of religion for his own political ends. He wants, in short, to control God.

➢ Undoubtedly there are leaders around today with the same end in view, and for this reason the relationship between the Church and the state is always delicate. As a Church we must take any opportunity offered to be involved in public life and decision-making at local or national level, but we must avoid being 'in the pocket' of any political group or leader.

➢ Cursing other people, or groups, is also still with us. Many, if not all, Caribbean islands still have their 'obeah' men or women, who will, if the price is right, put a curse on one's enemies. On a number of occasions in both St. Vincent and Grenada, Andrew was asked for help by people who believed they had been the victims of just this sort of evil activity.

Herod's interest in Jesus was similarly shallow; he had heard of this miracle worker and desired to see him, not, we are told, to discover Jesus' message or mission, but because he 'hoped to see him perform some sign'. In this, he too treated God as little more than a plaything, an object of curiosity, even idle self-interest. Tim Rice's words from *Jesus Christ, Superstar* have fixed Herod in many of our minds as an eccentric, even mad, buffoon, asking Jesus to

> prove to me that you're no fool – walk across my swimming pool,

feed my household with this bread – you can do it on your head,
prove to me that you're divine, turn my water into wine!

➤ We live in a world which, despite its consumerism and materialism, is nevertheless obsessed with the supernatural. Manifestations of psychic phenomena are big business; many adult magazines have adverts for 'Psychic tarot', 'Live clairvoyant spiritual psychic readings' and similar experiences. Like Herod, many people today want to see signs and wonders. Whilst we do and must believe in a God of miracles, a God who can and still does heal, who restores and reconciles us in body, mind and spirit, our gospel message does not stand or fall by these manifestations; for we, like Paul, 'proclaim Christ crucified, a stumbling-block to Jews and foolishness to Gentiles' (I Corinthians 1:23).

On a personal level, too, there may be times when our discipleship of Jesus has been little more than curiosity or self-interest:

➤ We have been drawn to gatherings which have offered a sensational revelation of God's power, but we have become faint-hearted in our daily walk with Christ.

➤ We have marvelled at the biographies of 'super-Christians' and wondered why we don't see such happenings in our local church, but we have not been willing to take up the cross of self-denial and even suffering.

➤ We have prayed only when we were in a mess and wanted God to 'click his fingers' and straighten things out for us, but we have forgotten to come back to God in thankful prayer when life is better.

➤ We have read the Bible hoping to find a ready solution to a current dilemma, but have neglected the daily discipline of Bible study.

➤ We have attended worship hoping that it will buy us God's favour in a difficult situation, forgetting that worship is the surrendering of self to a God who is worthy of all our praise.

➢ We have received Communion when we felt in need of a touch of power for a specific problem, not in utter humility as guests of a generous host.

Thankfully, God does not write us off because our motives are not always pure. As we come to him, he welcomes us and he is gracious in his response to our needs. We must beware, however, of trying to make God say what we want him to say (as Balak did) or do what we want him to do (as Herod wished), for in such times we may find him, as they did, to be silent, or even to say the very opposite of what we expect. Let us not forget that God is Sovereign, that Jesus Christ is Lord.

> **O Love divine, what hast thou done!**
>   **The immortal God hath died for me!**
> **The Father's co-eternal Son**
>   **Bore all my sins upon the tree;**
> **The immortal God for me hath died!**
> **My Lord, my Love is crucified –**
>
> **Is crucified for me and you,**
>   **To bring us rebels back to God;**
> **Believe, believe the record true,**
>   **We all are bought with Jesus' blood,**
> **Pardon for all flows from his side:**
> **My Lord, my Love is crucified.**
>
> **Then let us stand beneath the cross,**
>   **And feel his love a healing stream,**
> **All things for him account but loss,**
>   **And give up all our hearts to him;**
> **Of nothing think or speak beside:**
> **My Lord, my Love is crucified.**

Charles Wesley
HP 175

Prayer:

Lord God, you made me and you know me 'right well'. Thank you that in your presence I can shed all the masks of my life, knowing that you still accept me and even love me. I confess that at times my desire for control has even extended to how I view you and how I conduct my relationship with you. Humble me, I pray, in these last few days of Lent, that I may be raised with you in new life and power, for the sake of Jesus Christ. Amen

Maundy Thursday

Luke 22:54-62 &
Genesis 32: 6-8; 24-31

Fear

Then they seized [Jesus] and led him away, bringing him into the high priest's house. But Peter was following at a distance. When they had kindled a fire in the middle of the courtyard and sat down together, Peter sat among them. Then a servant-girl, seeing him in the firelight, stared at him and said, 'This man also was with him.' But he denied it, saying, 'Woman, I do not know him.' A little later someone else, on seeing him, said, 'You also are one of them.' But Peter said, 'Man, I am not!' Then about an hour later still another kept insisting, 'Surely this man also was with him; for he is a Galilean.' But Peter said, 'Man, I do not know what you are talking about!' At that moment, while he was still speaking, a cock crowed. The Lord turned and looked at Peter. Then Peter remembered the word of the Lord, how he had said to him, 'Before the cock crows today, you will deny me three times.' And he went out and wept bitterly.

The messengers returned to Jacob, saying, 'We came to your brother Esau, and he is coming to meet you, and four hundred men are with him.' Then Jacob was greatly afraid and distressed; and he divided the people that were with him, and the flocks and herds and camels, into two companies, thinking, 'If Esau comes to one company and destroys it, then the company that is left will escape.' . . .

. . . Jacob was left alone; and a man wrestled with him until daybreak. When the man saw that he did not prevail against Jacob, he struck him on the hip socket; and Jacob's hip was put out of joint as he wrestled with him. Then he said, 'Let me go, for the day is breaking.' But Jacob said, 'I will not let you go, unless you bless me.'

So he said to him, 'What is your name?' And he said, 'Jacob.' Then the man said, 'You shall no longer be called Jacob, but Israel, for you have striven with God and with humans, and have prevailed.' Then Jacob asked him, 'Please tell me your name.' But he said, 'Why is it that you ask my name?' And there he blessed him. So Jacob called the place Peniel, saying, 'For I have seen God face to face and yet my life is preserved.' The sun rose upon him as he passed Penuel, limping because of his hip.

➤ **Jacob had good cause** to be fearful of his brother. Years before he had cheated Esau out of the blessing due to him as the first-born of the twin brothers. Esau had made it quite clear that he intended to kill Jacob, so Jacob had fled many miles away and made a life for himself in the lands of his uncle, Laban. Now, with the considerable wealth and family he has amassed, he is returning to his homeland, wondering what sort of reception his brother, Esau, will have in store for him.

➤ **Peter had good cause** to be fearful. For the past three years he had been the right-hand man of someone who is now a notorious criminal. Jesus has been arrested and dragged away by the temple police. Somehow Peter scrapes together enough courage to follow Jesus, to stay as close as he can, and he loiters in the high priest's courtyard, warming himself in those dark minutes and hours of this nightmare.

➤ **Should Jacob have known better?** Years before, as he made his escape to Paddan-aram, he had had a remarkable vision of God in the place now known as Bethel. There God had promised, unconditionally, to bless him and to bring him back to his homeland (Genesis 28:10-22). Perhaps, like many of us, Jacob could not easily accept this offer of free grace, for he had responded by making a solemn vow, pledging that, if this should all come to pass, then the Lord would be his God.

> ➤ **Should Peter have known better?** He, of all the disciples, seems to have grasped first that Jesus was far more than a teacher, that he was God's Messiah. Earlier that very same day, Jesus had spoken urgent words to Peter individually: 'I have prayed for you that your own faith may not fail' (Luke 22:32); Peter in his turn had pledged his undying support for Jesus even should that lead to prison and death. Yet, when a mere servant-girl questions him about his association with Jesus he denies it totally.

> ➤ **What followed for Jacob** is one of the most remarkable encounters with God in the whole of Scripture. In the lonely darkness of the night, a man wrestles with him; who this man is, Jacob does not know, until, as the night ends, the stranger blesses him. Jacob concludes, as he lies in the dust of his own confusion, fear and injury, that 'I have seen God face to face, and yet my life is preserved' (Genesis 32:30). In the dawn of a new day, limping, he rises from the encounter and goes out to meet his brother – a meeting of peace and friendship in which God's promises to him are fulfilled.

> ➤ **What followed for Peter** was also a face-to-face meeting with God. As the words of his third denial echo around the courtyard, a cock crows, a new day is dawning for Peter too, and Jesus turns and looks at his friend. Bitterly ashamed, Peter goes out and weeps. That, thank God, is not the end of Peter's story, however. Through the grace of Jesus, offered to him in yet another dawn encounter just a few days later, (John 21:15-19) Peter also rises and, in the days to come, meets head-on the authorities of whom he had been so afraid. With great boldness he proclaims the gospel of Jesus, and fulfills Jesus' words to him, *'and you, once you have turned back, strengthen your brothers'* (Luke 22:32).

> ➤ **We have good cause to be fearful**, we may think, as we look around the world. The powers of darkness are alive and well; in many parts of the world, the Church is

declining as the spread of consumerism and secularism deadens the spirituality of whole nations. In countries where the Church is growing, it is often persecuted – directly or indirectly – governments do not always want to hear the voice of truth; international economic policy does not want to be hampered by justice or integrity. Youth culture is so fast-changing that few of us feel we can keep up, and the age profile of our congregations reflects an ever-widening 'culture-chasm' between young and old.

➢ **Should we know better?** What has Jesus said about the 'success' of his mission, about the security of his Church? As with Jacob and with Peter, he knows that we will often fail him, he has predicted hard times, troubles and persecutions (Matthew 24:9-13) yet he has entrusted us with his message and assured us of ultimate victory: 'I tell you, you are Peter, and on this rock I will build my church, and the gates of Hades will not prevail against it' (Matthew 16:18).

➢ **What can follow** our times of failure and denial; those opportunities to speak out or stand up for Christ on which we turn our backs for fear of mockery, fear of persecution, fear of indifference? From these two stories, and so many more in the pages of the Bible, we see that in our weakest, most fearful moments, God does not turn from us, but draws near to us, wanting to strengthen us to face those fears. Jacob received an injury; Peter knew bitter tears of shame – we too may find it painful as we meet God face to face, but in that pain is our healing.

> **'Tis Love! 'Tis Love! Thou diedst for me!**
> **I hear thy whisper in my heart;**
> **The morning breaks, the shadows flee,**
> **Pure, universal love thou art;**
> **To me, to all, thy mercies move:**
> **Thy nature and thy name is Love.**

My prayer has power with God;
the grace Unspeakable I now receive;
Through faith I see thee face to face,
I see thee face to face, and live!
In vain I have not wept and strove:
Thy nature and thy name is Love.

Charles Wesley
HP 434

Prayer:

Lord Jesus, I have stood by the fire with Peter, warming myself, and felt the cold chill of fear down my spine as someone has challenged my love for you, my faith in you, my commitment to you. Like Jacob I have run away from the threats of evil and disaster within society. Give me grace to look into your face today, to receive your forgiveness and to go out into your world in your strength and courage. Amen

Good Friday

John 19:16-20 & Genesis 22:1-8
Obedience

Then [Pilate] handed him over to them to be crucified. So they took Jesus; and carrying the cross by himself, he went out to what is called The Place of the Skull, which in Hebrew is called Golgotha. There they crucified him, and with him two others, one on either side, with Jesus between them. Pilate also had an inscription written and put on the cross. It read, 'Jesus of Nazareth, the King of the Jews.' Many of the Jews read this inscription, because the place where Jesus was crucified was near the city; and it was written in Hebrew, in Latin, and in Greek.

After these things God tested Abraham. He said to him, 'Abraham!' And he said, 'Here I am.' He said, 'Take your son, your only son Isaac, whom you love, and go to the land of Moriah, and offer him there as a burnt-offering on one of the mountains that I shall show you.' So Abraham rose early in the morning, saddled his donkey, and took two of his young men with him, and his son Isaac; he cut the wood for the burnt offering, and set out and went to the place in the distance that God had shown him. On the third day Abraham looked up and saw the place far away. Then Abraham said to his young men, 'Stay here with the donkey; the boy and I will go over there; we will worship, and then we will come back to you.' Abraham took the wood of the burnt-offering and laid it on his son Isaac, and he himself carried the fire and the knife. So the two of them walked on together. Isaac said to his father Abraham, 'Father!' And he said, 'Here I am, my son.' He said, 'The fire and the wood are here, but where is the lamb for a burnt-offering?' Abraham said, 'God himself will provide the lamb for a burnt-offering, my son.' So the two of them walked on together.

In the world-famous Passion Play, presented every ten years in the Austrian village of Oberammagau, the story of the last week of Jesus' life is vividly re-enacted. From time to time, an inner curtain is opened to reveal a tableau representing a scene from the Old Testament which has some bearing on the current action in Jesus' Passion. As Jesus makes his way to Golgotha, stumbling under the weight of the heavy wooden crossbar, so painful against his flayed and bleeding back, a tableau is revealed of the boy Isaac, walking with his father Abraham to Moriah, and bearing on his back the bundle of wood which is intended to become his funeral pyre.

Despite this parallel, the two stories end very differently – Isaac is spared as God speaks to Abraham telling him not to kill his son after all, and a ram is provided instead. For Jesus, however, there is no last-minute reprieve; Jesus knew that was possible for God, but impossible for God's purposes: 'Do you think that I cannot appeal to my Father, and he will at once send me more than twelve legions of angels? But how then would the scriptures be fulfilled, which say it must happen in this way?' (Matthew 26:53-54).

Both stories show us remarkable examples of obedience. Abraham had waited a very long time for his beloved son, Isaac, through whom he believed God would fulfil his promise to Abraham that he would become a great nation, the recipient and channel of great blessing. It made no sense for God to order the sacrifice of this young man, Isaac, and yet Abraham appears to make no protest, no excuse, no bargain; he simply sets out to obey God's instructions. The writers of the gospels give us a little more insight into the internal struggles of Jesus when called upon to offer himself up to death. As Jesus prays in Gethsemane, he asks if it be possible that this fearful cup of painful death might pass from him. Yet his obedience conquers his dread: 'Yet not what I want but what you want' (Matthew 26:39). In John's account Jesus says, 'Now my soul is troubled. And what should I say – "Father, save me from this hour"? No, it is for this reason that I have come to this hour. Father, glorify your name' (John 12:27).

Such words are not easy to say, yet they are vital if God's purposes are to be fulfilled and God is to be glorified in our lives. Ultimately, our love for Christ is shown not in our knowledge of the Bible, our attendance at, or fervour in, worship, the length of our private prayer time or our service for others, but in our obedience to his will. The Methodist Covenant prayer which we looked at last week sums this up:

> in some [services] we may please Christ and please ourselves;
> in others we cannot please Christ except by denying ourselves.

Those are the times which test our obedience, the times when we cannot please Christ except by denying ourselves. This is not a popular message today. I have a good friend who repudiates the custom of giving something up for Lent, because, she says, she cannot believe in a God of 'giving up'. Certainly we must beware of trivialising obedience to the extent that it means nothing more than going without biscuits or chocolate for a few weeks of the year. Obedience in both these stories is a matter of life or death.

> ➤ God's call upon our life may involve a radical cut in our level of disposable income – can we obey?

> ➤ God's purposes for us may mean we have to leave a much-loved place and move into the unknown. Saying goodbye to family and friends in order to move into a strange new world is never easy – can we obey?

> ➤ God's demands for holiness may mean we turn our back on a relationship which we know is playing with fire – can we obey?

> ➤ God's longing to reach out to the despised and rejected in society may involve us in going to places and speaking to people we have shunned – can we obey?

➤ God's commitment to faithfulness may mean we continue giving love and service in what seems to be a dead-end situation – can we obey?

In one sense, the Old and New Testament passages above are not different stories at all, but the beginning and ending of the same story. 'God himself will provide the lamb', Abraham tells his son, Isaac.

➤ This happens generations before the exodus of Israel from Egypt, when the blood of a lamb smeared on the doorposts of Hebrew houses saves the family within from disaster;

➤ This happens centuries before God establishes the sacrificial system, when the blood of lambs and other animals can secure forgiveness for his people's sins;

➤ This happens two millennia before Jesus himself comes in fulfilment of Abraham's words. God himself provides the lamb, his own well-beloved Son, offered as a sacrifice in Isaac's place and in our place.

> **Bearing shame and scoffing rude,**
> **In my place condemned he stood;**
> **Sealed my pardon with his blood:**
> **Alleluia! What a Saviour!**
>
> **Guilty, vile and helpless we;**
> **Spotless Lamb of God was he:**
> **Full atonement – can it be?**
> **Alleluia! What a Saviour!**

Philipp Bliss
HP 228

Prayer:

Lord Jesus Christ, thank you for your obedience to the will of your Father, which allows me to know God's love for me and God's forgiveness for my sin. Strengthen me, I pray, that in moments of rebellion, I too may humbly obey your will for my life, trusting you in all things, however difficult the task ahead may seem. Amen

Holy Saturday

Luke 23:52-56 &
Song of Solomon 2:10-13 & 3:1-3
Love

This man [Joseph of Arimathea] went to Pilate and asked for the body of Jesus. Then he took it down, wrapped it in a linen cloth, and laid it in a rock-hewn tomb where no one had ever been laid. It was the day of Preparation, and the sabbath was beginning. The women who had come with him from Galilee followed, and they saw the tomb and how his body was laid. Then they returned, and prepared spices and ointments. On the sabbath they rested according to the commandment.

My beloved speaks and says to me:
'Arise, my love, my fair one, and come away;
for now the winter is past,
the rain is over and gone.
The flowers appear on the earth;
the time of singing has come,
and the voice of the turtle-dove
is heard in our land.
The fig tree puts forth its figs,
and the vines are in blossom;
they give forth fragrance.
Arise my love, my fair one
and come away . . .
. . . Upon my bed at night
I sought him whom my soul loves;
I sought him, but found him not;
I called him, but he gave no answer.
'I will rise now and go about the city,
in the streets and in the squares;
I will seek him whom my soul loves.'
I sought him, but found him not.
The sentinels found me,
as they went about in the city.
'Have you seen him whom my soul loves?'

Our Lenten journey has touched on many themes and strands in our Christian discipleship. One theme, one motivation, has surfaced again and again, and if the story of Christ's life, suffering and death can be summed up in one word it is 'love'.

➢ In Luke's Gospel especially we can find a consistent thread telling of the women who followed Jesus. Rarely in the limelight, but almost always somewhere in the picture, this small group of women defied convention and perhaps risked censure in order to remain close to Jesus. Their love for him is unaltered by his death; still they wait in the wings and watch, preparing to do whatever can be done — even if all that is to anoint his dead body.

➢ The Song of Solomon draws the poignant picture of a girl, summoned by her lover, celebrating with him the potency and passion of spring; then finding herself alone in the night. The lover is gone; she calls him but he does not answer, so she goes out into the city to seek him. She spends no time calculating what her response should be, or weighing up the pros and cons of various possible courses of action; she reacts out of an overwhelming love for her beloved.

On this last day of Lent we may want to consider: what is our chief motivation for following Christ?

A mental commitment to what we believe is true and right?
    The hope of heaven?
        The fear of hell?
           Duty?
                Tradition?
                Habit?
                    Or love, overwhelming, vulnerable love?

My God, I love thee – not because
I hope for heaven thereby,
Nor yet because who love thee not
Are lost eternally.

Thou, O my Jesus, thou didst me
Upon the cross embrace;
For me didst bear the nails and spear,
And manifold disgrace;

And griefs and torments numberless,
And sweat of agony,
Yea, death itself, and all for one
Who was thine enemy.

Then why, O blessèd Jesus Christ,
Should I not love thee well?
Not for the sake of winning heaven;
Nor of escaping hell;

Not with the hope of gaining aught,
Not seeking a reward;
But as thyself hast lovèd me,
O ever-loving Lord!

E'en so I love thee, and will love,
And in thy praise will sing;
Solely because thou art my God
and my eternal King.

17th Century
tr. Edward Caswall
HP 171

'The love of God constrains us' (2 Corinthians 5:14 KJV) is the motto of the Methodist Church in the Caribbean and the Americas. In the islands of the Caribbean and in these islands of Britain, I have met many people for whom that has been a personal motto, people whose varying motives have been overruled by that love:

➤ A Sunday School teacher who has, through the constraining love of Christ, overcome **jealousy** of another's gifts in order to work alongside that person and bring the love of God to a group of children.

➤ A skilled electrician who, ignoring the opportunities for **personal gain** through private commissions, gave endless hours and innumerable materials for the building of a new church in a needy community.

➤ A woman who has recognised her dependency on alcohol as a **weakness** and has learned to lean daily upon the strength of Christ.

➤ A church council which has surrendered its desire to **control** the direction of the church, and even to control the way God is at work in that congregation, and instead has become open to God's guidance and empowering.

➤ A young woman who has not allowed **fear** of her colleagues' comments or her family's mockery to deflect her from God's calling to preach the gospel.

Personally, I often feel very lacking in love – in my own strength I cannot even love those closest to me, let alone those who (thank God) differ from me in so many ways. In Chateaubelair in 1994-95 I experienced a revelation (and revolution) of love which changed my life. God is never lacking in love and can supply the love we need today and every day – love for ourselves, love for those around us, love for those far away from us, and love for God. As we wait and watch during this last night of darkness, this last night of our Lenten vigil, like the women of our gospel passage, we are preparing to serve Jesus in whatever way we can. Unlike them, we know that in a blaze of joy and light tomorrow morning, we shall meet our Risen Lord.

> **Lo, Jesus meets us, risen from the tomb;**
> **Lovingly he greets us, scatters fear and gloom;**
> **Let the church with gladness hymns of triumph sing,**
> **For her Lord now liveth, death hath lost its sting.**

Edmond Budry,
tr. Richard Hoyle
HP 212

Acknowledgements

Scripture quotations are from the New Revised Standard Version of the Bible, Anglicized Edition, copyright © 1989, 1995 by the Division of Christian Education of the National Council of the Churches of Christ in the USA.

Page

46   C. S. Lewis, *The Lion, the Witch and the Wardrobe,* Puffin Books, Penguin. © Estate of C. S. Lewis 1950. Permission applied for.

88   C. S. Lewis, *Prince Caspian,* Puffin Books, Penguin. © Estate of C. S. Lewis 1951. Permission applied for.

104   Steven Croft, 'Pierce my ear', CopyCare, PO Box 77, Hailsham, East Sussex, BN27 3EF. Permission applied for.

107   Richard Gillard, 'Brother, Sister, let me serve you', Sovereign Music UK. Permission applied for.

116   T. S. Colvin, 'Jesu, Jesu, fill us with your love', Stainer & Bell Ltd. Permission applied for.

136-37 'King Herod's Song' from *Jesus Christ Superstar*
Lyrics by Tim Rice
Music by Andrew Lloyd Webber
© copyright 1970 The Really Useful Group Ltd., London. All Rights Reserved. International Copyright Secured. Used by permission.